PRACTICAL GUIDE TO
DOGS

Hamlyn
London · New York · Sydney · Toronto

PRACTICAL GUIDE TO DOGS

Kay White · Joan Joshua

Acknowledgements

With the exception of those listed below all the photographs in this book were supplied by Anne Cumbers who wishes to thank the following owners for their kind co-operation:
Mrs Baker; Mrs Baxter; Mrs Booth, Mrs Bowers; Mr Bradley; Miss Casson; Mrs Cooke; Mrs Coy; Mrs Crawley; Mrs Derring; Mrs Dobson; Mrs Ford; P Gibbs; Hilary Harmar; Mrs Heron, Farron Hill; Mrs Howard; Mrs Hutchinson; Mrs Hutton; Colin Hyde; Mrs Jackson; Joan Joshua; Mrs Mahoney; Mrs Miller; Mrs Platt; Mrs Preston; Mrs Robinson; A Sayer; Francis Spear; Mrs Speat; Mrs Stringer; Mrs Tidley; Pamela Turle; Mrs Turrell; Kay White; Marilyn Willis; Mr and Mrs Wolf; Mr and Mrs Young.

Other colour illustrations
M K Boorer 59 bottom; R N Chambers 102 bottom; Neil Curtis 50 top, 58 top (with acknowledgement to Howard and Ellen Curtis); *Daily Telegraph* 71; Keystone 98 bottom; Syndication International 23; Harold White 19 bottom (with acknowledgement to Kay White).

Other black and white illustrations
Peter Ayling 16 (with acknowledgement to Kay White); Will Green 6; Harold White 2 (by permission of Bailliere Tindall), 73; Thomas A Wilkie 85.

Line drawings by Harold White.

Published by The Hamlyn Publishing Group Limited
London · New York · Sydney · Toronto
Astronaut House, Feltham, Middlesex, England
Copyright © The Hamlyn Publishing Group Limited 1975

Reprinted 1978

ISBN 0 600 37046 1

Phototypeset by Tradespools Limited, Frome, Somerset

Printed and bound in Spain
by Graficromo, S. A. – Córdoba

Contents

Introduction

The dog has always been a clever creature, well aware of where its best opportunities would lie. It has used its superb nose, eyes, and ears and its keen brain to make a success of the species while others have been struggling to survive. The dog was born to be a roving pack animal, but very early on saw that it would do better to live close to man, and that is what it has been doing, in varying capacities, since prehistoric times. Dog's natural rôle as a pack animal renders it suitable for domination by a stronger animal which has larger brain capacity and more cunning. The dog is eminently suitable to adapt to the many functions which man has demanded from it, altering in temperament, size, colour, coat texture, and character. In return, dog has earned food, shelter, and companionship in varying degrees which reach their peak at the present time when pet dog care provides big industry in many countries.

Horses of all breeds look similar, as do cats, but it is surprising to realize that the mastiff and the chihuahua, the terrier, the beagle, the spaniel, and the pug all derive from the same ancestry. They are all dogs. Not only do they look and feel different, but they have different talents and abilities. The dog breeds we know today have been created by man for specific purposes, by breeding to shape, colour, and ability, and the process still goes on, as show breeders strive to improve their stock for particular points.

Dog's relationship with man began in prehistoric times, when it would help to herd reindeer which were kept as milk and meat providers. It would also guard the settlement against enemies and predators. Dog also made itself useful at hunting game, retrieving, and pulling down heavy animals which man could then kill. The courage to attack, and turn of speed made the dog less liable to injury than its master, and it was clearly a useful asset to a primitive culture. Dog found this way of life agreeable, too. It would seem, from evidence we have of cave drawings and entombed skeletons, that dog was always able to endear itself to man, not only for its useful qualities, but for its beauty and devotion. The packs of dogs that surrounded settlements began to disband and attach themselves as individuals, and dog found that there were even more rôles to play. It could be a companion and plaything for children, a confidant and comforter to the lonely, a hot water bottle for the chilly, a waste disposal unit for bits of gristle, an adornment for a lovely lady, or an attribute for a handsome gallant.

Thousands of years later we have more dogs than ever, but few of them earn their livings at all except in the more vicarious

A portion of a veterinary papyrus of Kahun 1900 B.C.

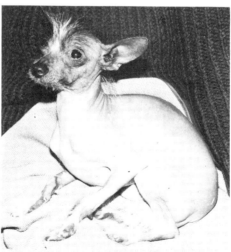

The Mexican hairless dog is not recognized by the British or American Kennel Clubs. The high body temperature of this breed was once considered helpful as a relief for rheumatism and kidney disorders.

A trained guide dog in harness safely guiding her blind master across a busy road.

The German shepherd dog here is demonstrating agility and obedience to his owner's command in this long-jump exercise, which is part of the working trial requirements.

ways of fulfilling our needs as pets. Some use their talents for steadiness and obedience as guide dogs for the blind, their noses as police and excise department dogs, or their natural possessiveness as guard dogs. Most just use their amiability to provide us with fun and friendship. Their similarity to human physiology, and the ability some breeds still retain to live in the pack make them suitable as experimental animals. Many drugs are tested, and pilot operations carried out on dogs which live in colonies maintained by pharmaceutical companies. In this way, as in all the others, the dog continues to serve.

The domesticated dog today is totally dependent upon us for every facet of its life,

but despite appearances the dog is still basically a wild animal. The bitch at the peak of her season for mating, the frustrated male, the terrified animal, or the unruly dog making a bid to be the dominant personality in the home can all be very close to the uncontrollable wild creature. Any dog can be vicious, destructive, and wild. Whatever your breed choice, it is important to understand how the dog pack hierarchy operates, so that you may always be the master, and in a position to command obedience without the necessity for bullying and ugly scenes. The dog is conditioned to submit to a pack leader, and you have to be sure that the leader is you, never forgetting that an uncontrollable pekingese can be just as trying as a bigger dog. Both can prove such a nuisance that you may end by taking the potentially dangerous, subordinate position or the sad course of having the dog destroyed because you failed in the early training.

Dogs living in a group submit to, and acknowledge their leader, the strongest character which by sheer force of will rules the others. Physical strength is not important. In my own boxer pack the leader has always been a bitch, not necessarily the eldest, and always smaller than the males, which respect her even more than do the females. When we have had a strong, dominant pack leader there have been few fights among the underlings, and they are generally more easy to control in every way.

The pack leader will express disapproval if a young dog breaks household rules, or defies a human, even though it is not above breaking a few rules itself. When the pack leader has not been a strong enough personality, or has identified itself too closely with humans, we have had periodic fights, expecially among the bitches of young middle-age which have ambition to rise to the top. Such animals are capable of fighting to kill among themselves, and yet are able to withdraw at once if they feel their teeth sink into human flesh. The dog that is willing to bite man is usually a fear-biter – either unbalanced mentally, or having suffered some experience so grievous that it cannot forgive. The dog that bites without provocation has no place in society today, and should certainly never be passed on as a guard dog. Breeds with natural guarding potential never have to use their teeth except on dog biscuit, and only the stupid will encourage or incite them to attack, even in play.

Dogs rely heavily on human companionship, especially those dogs which were bred to do a job and are now unemployed. The boxer, the Old English sheepdog, the basset hound, the beagle, were created for specific purposes and feel frustrated alone in a small house. If they cannot do the work their instincts crave, they must at least have companionship of a human or one of their own kind to save them from boredom and claustrophobia. It is an extreme unkindness to have a dog if you expect to leave it alone several hours each day. Its intelligence is too high to survive this treatment without getting into mischief and doing damage for which you can only blame yourself.

We rate a dog's brain capacity quite high in the animal kingdom; they are capable of understanding a range of words and tone inflections, and of anticipating your actions. All the same, we are taking into our households an animal, and it would be wrong to try to mould it into a mini-human, or substitute child, and to seek to obliterate all its natural characteristics. Dogs behave instinctively in ways that are unacceptable or embarrassing to humans, but to attempt to stop these behaviour patterns will turn your dog into a neurotic wreck. However much your dog may relate to you, it must also maintain communication with its own species, even if it is never able to meet them. Dogs communicate with each other by

Pack leader expresses domination behaviour to a young bitch which in turn demonstrates homage. This ritual takes place daily after which they both lie happily together.

roll over and expose its genitals for investigation, saying, in effect, 'bite me if you will'. The well-conditioned, dominant dog will accept this surrender in a cool manner. Over-interference by owners in this initial encounter stage can precipitate a fight which would never have happened if the dogs were left to work it out for themselves. Size and breed may have little effect on the outcome; a large breed puppy will acknowledge the superiority of a small, mature dog. Panicking by the owners serves to aggravate a situation that the dogs have perfectly under control. Dogs that acknowledge each other as of equal status and of no sexual interest may then pass amicably on. There may be the traditional invitation to play, front legs at the crouch, hind legs bent to spring, or there may be the deliberate aversion of the head, tension of the body, that means a trial of wills to come.

A dominant pack leader accepts homage from its underlings, a ritualized performance in which they abase themselves before the leader, heads low, rear ends high, licking at the face and lips. The pack leader's response is a lip-curling snarl and roar, with neck extended, and sometimes a paw placed on the lower dog to emphasize the need to grovel. Some breeds, notably the Labrador retriever, greet their owners with the 'lip-curl' movement, a mimic of the human smile. Underdogs are not allowed to confront the leader head-on; you will notice the approach from the side, with head averted. All these movements, born into the species, are practised by puppies at play from the age of four weeks, and good canine mothers go on to teach their pups the basics of submission, defence mechanisms, and methods of attack.

Dog psychologists have found that the best way for a pup to be conditioned to life with human beings is to remove it from the nest at six weeks of age. While the dog may adjust more easily to domestic conditions by this method it also deprives it of canine companionship and nursery schooling in being a dog, which it should learn from its mother. The result may be a maladjusted dog which is atypical of its breed. The ideal solution is to take the very young puppy into a home where it can live with, or often meet, other dogs.

Urinating has far more importance for a dog than just emptying the bladder. Males in particular mark out their territory and

means of scent, facial and body expression, physical contact, and barking and whining noises in that order. Even the dogs with short noses, which are not expected to have high scenting ability, are far more sensitive to smells than is man.

It is thought that each dog carries an individual scent, mainly emanating from the rectum and genital area. By mutual nose to tail investigation a dog not only recognizes friend or foe, but also the state of their health, temper, and libido. Certainly, this traditional approach is one of inquiry. If the scent response is not congenial, the hackles (the hair along the ridge of the back) will begin to stand erect and the body will stiffen. This is a primeval device to make the animal look larger and more fierce than it naturally is, probably initiated by an upsurge of adrenalin, the fight or flight syndrome. The submissive dog will lower its head, probably things under their ownership. Bitches urinate more frequently when they are coming into oestrus, in order to spread the news. Many bitches will normally only use their own gardens, to the frustration of owners who will have walked them great distances only to find she waits until she gets home. But if she has a message to pass, only then will she use strange territory.

The bitch habit of being very particular where she urinates can be a trial on holiday or when she is in boarding kennels, when she may restrain herself for forty-eight hours or more in the hope of getting back to familiar territory. A bitch with absolutely exemplary house training will sometimes urinate on her owners' clothing, bed, or pillow when in a stress situation. It would seem that the act of urinating on something that has been close to the owner reinforces a sense of belonging to the family. This has happened with my dogs once or twice when they have been left in a hotel room when we have gone down to dinner. I think it must mean that they were disoriented or frightened, because any normal lapse of house cleanliness will be performed as near the exit door as possible.

All puppies and bitches urinate in a squatting position. The adult male mostly raises one hind leg so that he may direct the urine at a chosen target, but when bladder emptying is more urgent than message giving he, too, will semi-squat. A very dominant pack leader bitch will sometimes try to elevate one leg into a male position. This probably indicates that she has an overbalance of male hormone in her make-up, giving her the necessary strong character for dominance.

Puppies and emotional bitches may urinate at extreme pleasure, when greeting their owner, or in fear. This demonstration of submission usually ceases as the dog grows up.

The male dog marks out his territory, and the area on which he is taken for exercise by directing a deliberate stream of urine, and should another dog have passed that way, he will endeavour to blot out the alien scent with his own. Dogs also tend to mark new objects brought into the household – christening the new broom or the garden chair once, and once only. We may feel it is totally reprehensible that our dog lifts his leg against the drawing room curtains when he has every opportunity to go outside, until we remember that we had a visitor with a male dog, or an in-season bitch. It would be wrong to inflict punishment for this instinctive behaviour, although we may show disapproval. The best way, however, would be to forestall the attempt before it can occur. The investigation of faeces left by other animals is also of great interest to the dog.

Most dogs will keep their feet and genitals spotlessly clean by licking, and bitches will take care of a lot of their discharge when in season. Dogs will also groom each other,

Traditional pose for an invitation to play with a human or another dog.

The challenge pose, accompanied by a growl, is an indication of a trial of strength to come.

Duck's Cottage Pixie showing clearly that a dog's natural dignity can be offended as easily as a human's

paying particular attention to the insides of ears, which may harbour some discharge. They will also attend to each other's wounds, even solicitously licking the bite they inflicted just before. Blood and suppurative discharges are naturally attractive to the dog, but if disapproval is shown, such licking is discouraged. A good dam will clean her puppies vigorously and consume all their excreta and urine until they are weaned. Some bitches and dogs will vomit partly digested food for their young. This is feral behaviour which fulfils a parental instinct in the dog and it should not be discouraged.

The dog scratches where it itches, without reserve; sometimes it will scratch where it does not itch as an expression of embarrassment or to distract the owner from other behaviour that the dog thinks may be wrong. It is interesting to see that thousands of years of association with man has induced in the dog guilt feelings which are rarely seen in other animals, certainly not in the cat.

Your pet may have torn up yesterday's newspaper, or a priceless first edition; it has no way of distinguishing, but it clearly knows when it has done wrong. The dog's intelligence, alas, does not always extend to preventing repetition of the fault.

Digging is an inbuilt skill, to make a lair in which to hide or whelp, to bury food, or to flush out prey. Man exploits the talent when he needs it, but takes exception to little pits dug all over the lawn. The pet dog making rudimentary attempts to follow the ways of its ancestors should be admonished but not punished, because lack of human supervision is the real cause of damage to the garden. The young dog will get into mischief as readily as the young child, and their misdemeanours may be treated with some parity.

The dog values physical contact, with its own kind, and with its owner. To stroke and to pat is a physical need in the human being, and the embraces which we may feel too inhibited to offer our fellow humans are readily accepted, even sought by the dog. It likes to press its sensitive nose against our warm skin, and to lick our hand, savouring our personal odour. An excess of this behaviour may be curbed, but the dog that is never allowed to snuggle or lean against its owner's legs is a deprived creature. Dogs living together will always sleep entwined, or at least, touching. This is because of the reinforcement of strength which comes from being part of the pack. Dog believes there is warmth and safety in numbers, and to be lonely is its most unhappy state.

Dogs often turn circles in their beds before settling down. Behavioural studies now indicate that this is done to flex the spine before going into the tight curl, nose to tail, in which the solitary dog sleeps, conserving its body heat. The young puppy sleeps flat, expecting that its fellows or its dam (mother) will provide a source of heat. Dogs dream just as people do; we have all seen them chasing the enemy, giving muffled barks, or kicking their legs while still deeply asleep.

All dogs can vary their bark, and the intuitive owner will soon learn to recognize the tones, as a mother may her baby's cries. The first purpose of barking is to warn the pack of approaching danger, nowadays perhaps the burglar or simply the postman. Oddly enough, few dogs learn to indicate when the telephone rings. This may be because the owner shows no sign of apprehension or excitement at this noise, or perhaps the bell tone is not shrill enough to alarm the dog, which regards it as part of ordinary household exchange. Most dogs bark at the door bell, even though they must be familiar with that noise, too, but they may sense more alarm in their owner's reaction to it.

The young puppy will play-bark from about four weeks, and will continue to play in noisy fashion throughout adolescence. Those not actively engaged in the game will bark from the side lines, cheering on their mates, and inciting them to further effort, just like a football crowd. Intelligence in adaptation is evidenced by the dog that teaches itself to bark when it wants to come in or go out, or wants food – this communication with its owner can also be taught quite easily by example. If you bark at a puppy, very soon it barks back. It is more difficult to stop the yapping of the smaller breeds which seems instinctive to them and yet serves no useful purpose.

Like people, some dogs are less inhibited with the voice than others and, of course, the working hound breeds and terriers were encouraged to give tongue when performing their proper function. If we keep these breeds as pets then that instinct has to be trained out. In the last resort a veterinary surgeon can perform a debarking operation. The dog confined in an outhouse, or put into boarding kennels may 'protest bark' for many hours; others will attempt to find a way out, some will sit in silent misery. It is the varying personalities that make dogs so interesting.

The howl, so much feared by humans as a bad luck omen, does not seem so doom laden to the dog. Howling may be a pack-rallying call, or mating message – howling carries much further than the bark, and is always given sitting or standing, never on the move. Some dogs find a combination of howl and whine noise easier than a bark, and use it for all purposes. The so-called barkless basenji uses this howl. The whine is the very first noise a puppy makes, and is always used on a supplicant note, asking for something in the nicest possible way. The growl and snarl are active warnings of further action to come unless the adversary gives in. It may be bluff, it is up to the owner to see that the dog never ends a growl session on the winning end.

Tail wagging is used to show pleasure or

A young dog of true guarding strain challenging intruders to his property.

to excite the dog to further activity – the growl at one end and the wag at the other indicating some uncertainty of future behaviour. The wagging tail may soon be tucked between the legs while the dog runs in fear. Dogs which have had their tails artificially docked will wag their spines in a curving movement of greeting.

The original strong guard instinct is in the pet dog turned into possessiveness about its own territory, car, bed, and toys. We feel proud that our dog guards us, but we must never let the instinct go too far. A dog has no moral sense in the human scale of values. If it finds a joint of meat unattended, the dog will take it, and such action is not 'stealing', it is taking advantage of a good opportunity afforded by someone's carelessness. Such booty which has come by quickness of nose and eye is always particularly prized and difficult to retrieve. Dogs have a deep sense of play and mischief, and love to tantalize their owner in the way they would their siblings in the pack. Bitches will guard their newborn pups with a ferocity which even their owners find difficult to understand. A bitch may forbid even well-loved members of the household to approach her box for the first few days after whelping, allowing only one chosen attendant. Extravagant guarding on the part of the bitch can result in her lying on the puppies, even killing them in an effort to protect them from what she considers danger. Unless conditions give her some basis for extreme fear, such a bitch is showing neurotic tendencies and should not be used for breeding purposes again.

The balanced guard dog, allowed a measure of responsibility and freedom, does not attack even when highly suspicious of a stranger. It stands erect, often positioning itself at the entrance to the premises, or across the body of its owner, so that it comes between owner or property and enemy. If the dog's warning is not heeded, and the owner shows or feels apprehension, the dog may spring at the adversary, take hold, and bring him down. The dog should not continue to bite. If you own such a powerful dog you must be able to control it at all times, and to be sure that you can call the dog off before it takes further aggressive action. A 'biter' is not a guard, it is a danger. The dog that backs away, snapping and biting through fear is showing its own incompetence to deal with a situation.

Some dogs are particularly sensitive about guarding their cars, perhaps because they feel vulnerable with glass all round them and attack liable to come from any side. The well-balanced guard is constantly on the alert, even when supposedly sleeping. It will raise its eyebrows at a noise, perhaps go to investigate and trot back plainly saying 'that's alright, nothing important'. The jittery dog that raises an alarm at every noise

This saluki, a traditional hunting breed, is showing affection for a kitten.

is not desirable, but may well be rendered this way by the owner who does not allow it the opportunity to see and assess the approaching enemy. If you rush the dog away every time visitors come it may conclude that everyone is evil, or in some way undesirable for it to meet. Owners are sometimes disappointed that their dogs, bought as guards, are too friendly in puppyhood. This is a good fault. Guard instinct does not make itself felt until the puppy is out of adolescence, perhaps at about two years old, when the animal would be establishing its place in the pack. Warning barking may well not start until this age also.

Dogs may be taught to live with any other species, and even to distinguish between the family pet rabbit and cat, and others that may be hunted. A hound and a fox have been brought up as litter mates, but those taking a hunting or a scenting breed into the home as pets must always remember that the basic instinct to chase or to follow a scent has to be trained out, or prevented by enclosure from which the dog cannot escape.

Dogs enjoy the company of their kind, whether the same or different breeds. There is no combination of large or small, terrier and toy, that cannot be made to work, but each may teach the other all the tricks of its kind, and you may have a chihuahua that hunts rabbits with its springer spaniel friend, and a Dane that wants to sit on your lap in the same way as the Maltese. Most dogs up to middle age will accept a puppy into the household, and will to some extent renew their youth in playing with the new arrival. Introductions must be tactfully made over a period of at least two weeks, and the animals must never be left unsupervised until they have, of their own volition, established body contact and play relationship. Sharing the same bed is a strong indication of acceptance of one another – studied ignoring of the newcomer may break down if they are left alone together. The balanced, mature dog will not harm a puppy fatally, but it might frighten it badly.

It is not kind to ask a very old dog to be bothered with a lively puppy which will give it no peace. Some equable breeds, the spaniels, for instance, will accept the introduction of adult dogs into the household. Possessive breeds such as the boxer, Dobermann, or pug will not accept another of the

Are you a dog too?

same sex, possibly no other dog at all. In an only pet situation, the puppy taken early from the nest may be absolutely devoted to its owner, totally dependent, and devastated when left alone. The pup must be gradually conditioned to being a dog for part of its time, and being excluded from some human activities. For example, during family mealtimes the dog should be in the kitchen rather than beside the owner's chair, or worse, sitting up to table. Such an animal may be so humanized as to refuse to mate with its own species, and to be in great fear of all other dogs, totally disoriented in both human and animal worlds. Such tendencies can be curbed in youth by allowing play with other animals and strong affection but not over-identification with any human being. Some owners seem unduly anxious for their puppy to show adult characteristics. They may worry that the male has not leg-raised to urinate, nor the bitch come into season. Like a human baby, a puppy needs to feel secure and loved but not stifled, it needs to have the limits of permitted behaviour clearly defined, and needs to know that some actions are not allowed but are not unforgivable. Both puppy and child need contact with their own kind, and with all the types of environment which they are likely to meet later. They need cushioning against rash, youthful behaviour by an experienced adult. Kindness, tolerance, and forethought are the best qualities for raising a pet to be a source of pleasure and pride.

Choosing your dog

With such variety in the canine species, somewhere there is probably the ideal dog for you. The family's relationship with its pet must be a love affair, however, not entirely an arrangement based on suitability. While in theory it is true to say that you must choose a dog that fits into the space, income, and time available, if you want to own any breed badly enough, you will make it possible to keep that dog. Even a Saint Bernard in a small flat is possible, if you make it your sole preoccupation, although no one could pretend that it was suitable or easy.

Your dog is going to be a major investment, not only of money and time, but emotion too, and the purchase demands a great deal of thought and discussion among all who are to be involved in its care. There must be great enthusiasm, particularly from those who are at home all day and likely to be in closest association with the dog. You should discuss the proposed purchase for months before a decision is made. It should be talked over not only on sunny days on country walks, but on wet Mondays in winter – what we should have to give up if we had a dog, rather than what we should gain. The pleasures are easy to assess, the nuisance value not always as apparent.

If you have a dog you cannot leave home easily, even for a half day trip. Families whose pleasure is caravanning or sailing, will have to consider how the dog is to fit in with their other interests and yet be given the companionship which it will need. Take your time before buying, and when you have made your choice, be prepared to wait for the right dog, perhaps even as long as six or eight months from breeders who are not simply concerned with financial gain. The impulse buy is almost always doomed to failure, because you will be very lucky to find top class stock of the right age just waiting for you to call.

The best place to buy your puppy is from a breeder who specializes in one or two breeds only, who can show you at least one of the parents of your puppy, and where you can judge for yourself the conditions in which the puppy has been reared up to the time you take it. Where a wide variety of puppies is advertised from one address you may be sure that they have been bought in from many different sources, and will probably have already made long, traumatic journeys. Such puppies start off with physical and temperamental handicaps.

In Britain breeders may be found through The Kennel Club, and throughout the world from equivalent canine associations and clubs, through weekly papers devoted to dog breeding and showing such as *Dog World* and *Our Dogs*, and through classified advertisements in local and weekly newspapers. You will also find that other pet owners are only too pleased to talk to you about their pets, and can tell you whether they were pleased with the services they received when they bought their puppy. It is sensible to contact breeders within reasonable distance of your home, so that you may easily return for advice. If there are no puppies available at the time, and you must wait, at least you will have the anticipatory thrill of seeing the pregnant dam, hearing about the birth, and choosing your puppy at the earliest possible moment. Given normal good health, dog's life expectancy ranges from seven years in some breeds to fifteen in others. This animal, then, is going to be part of the family, a permanent responsibility for a good number of years. The dog should never be regarded as a disposable possession, not only for its own sake, but for the sense of insecurity which children may feel if the dog is sent away when it is troublesome or inconvenient.

Most breeders will refuse to sell you a puppy as a surprise present; surprises do not always work out. Christmas is a most unsuitable time to take a new puppy because it needs to be started in its new home in an atmosphere of concentrated concern, not

Boxer puppies just ready to go to their new homes.

during a busy, exciting holiday. If the puppy is a planned present, give a puppy token such as a photograph, or a collar and lead, and then pick up the puppy which you have previously reserved when the festivities are over.

When you go to choose your puppy you should be quite certain what breed you want, and what sex. In the larger breeds especially, the behaviour and attitudes of males and females differ markedly. Among smaller dogs control is easier so that the sex chosen is not so important from that aspect. Bitches are no cheaper than male dogs; they may even be more expensive when their breeding potential is taken into account. Bitches are, in general, rather more loving and devoted, but they suffer from hormone-based mood swings at varying stages in their breeding cycle. Male dogs tend to be more out-going and interested in their own kind, but their temperament is more consistent.

It is great fun to buy two puppies at a time, if you have room. They will always be company for each other, and rather less charge on you; they will also be more of a pair of dogs than one humanized animal. It is very difficult indeed to keep a dog and bitch apart at the height of her season.

If you see a litter when it is about four weeks old, this is the earliest time it is really possible to make a reasoned choice. Remember little puppies do tire easily, and the one that looks sleepy now may have been playing excitedly ten minutes before you arrived. Perhaps the whole litter is lethargic and huddled together – not ill, just contented babies sleeping and growing. At six weeks

A healthy springer spaniel puppy showing excellent bone conformation.

old they will be far more animated and at eight weeks will readily respond to any stimulating action, even if they are resting. Make your choice with due regard to your requirements in a dog whether it be the loving, snuggly one, or the out-going, up-to-mischief one which is climbing out of the playpen. In a guarding breed do not take the boldest puppy unless you are confident that you can handle an animal which may make a bid for domination at some stage.

In many homes, a bitch of the guarding breeds will be as strong as most owners will want to handle. Try to resolve not to take the poor little puppy that you feel sorry for. Only strong and healthy puppies should be offered for sale, the price differential relating only to symmetry of marking and breed standard conformation. The puppy in poor health is never a bargain, and is better put down. Look for animated, bright eyes;

A dog with good conformation will be well up on the pasterns, with well-developed second thighs, and tail correctly set on for breed.

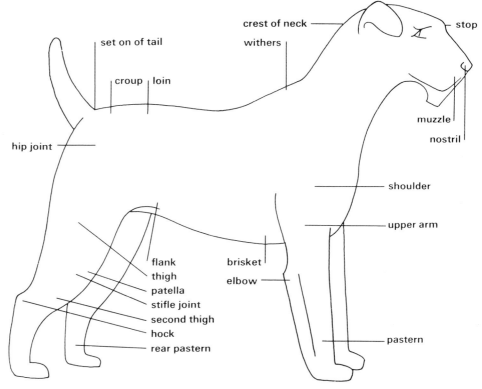

crest of neck

stop

withers

set on of tail

croup loin

muzzle

nostril

hip joint

shoulder

upper arm

flank
thigh
patella
stifle joint
second thigh
hock
rear pastern

brisket

elbow

pastern

healthy, pleasant smelling coat; clean skin and ears; well-formed excreta; and a full complement of sharp little teeth at eight weeks. Do not take a puppy with an inguinal hernia (a lump in the groin which will need an operation soon), and do not take a puppy for breeding with an umbilical hernia (a lump around the navel). These are hereditary faults.

If you are having a male puppy it is better to choose one with two testicles ready to descend into the scrotum. If you are planning to breed or show it is almost essential to have an entire male. You can get a veterinary opinion on this point. It is not always possible to be sure that a dog will be entire at puberty when you buy a puppy at eight or nine weeks, but the unilateral cryptorchid (one testicle) or the cryptorchid with none, may be at risk from disease in later life. Hormonal imbalance may also lead these imperfect males to temperamental disturbance. A dog with only one descended testicle can sire puppies, and should not be trusted with an in-season bitch.

The healthy puppy is heavy for its size but not fat, and it must not have a sagging belly. Do not tolerate runny eyes, diarrhoea, coughs, bare rims round the eyes, and pup-

pies which cannot move firmly on all four legs at eight weeks. Please disinfect your shoes and clothing before going on to the next address. A puppy which is noticeably smaller than its litter mates should be checked by a veterinary surgeon to make sure that no physical defect is inhibiting its growth.

Available dogs fall into four categories: the mongrel; the typed dogs which are not recognized by a kennel club, for example, in Britain the Jack Russell; the pedigreed puppy of the kennel club registered breeds; and the prospective show dog from those breeds. Your choice is again complicated by the question of getting a puppy or an adult. Young adult dogs may often be seen advertised as needing good new homes. Many breed clubs in Britain operate rescue sections to take into care unwanted specimens of their breed, and there are also the well-known dog rescue societies, with full kennels. You may also be able to buy from showing kennels a young animal which has not developed according to early promise, or a bitch which has finished her useful breeding life at about five years old. It is rewarding to feel that you are offering a home to a dog that would otherwise be displaced, and some

Above and left **The Pyrenean mountain dog and the long-haired dachshund show the range of size in the canine race.** *Right* **Other bitches, even friends, are not permitted to interfere with puppies.**

delightful pets are obtained in this way.

It would not be correct to say that to take an adult is going to save you trouble. You may get a ready made dog, but it is more than likely that a young adult being advertised has behavioural faults which have made it unacceptable to its first owners. A dog that has been unwanted, that has spent some time in kennels, is likely to need a refresher course in house-training; it will certainly need to be given time to become reoriented and adapt to your home. If you take an adult, be prepared for a strenuous month's work of rehabilitation. Some dogs that have always been kennelled never house-train reliably, and may never be particularly close as pets. Most families will want a puppy, to enjoy the baby days and to bring up to fit in with their life style. No one enjoys the house-training stage, but this is something that really must be done in the new home; it is a waste of money to pay a third party to house-train a puppy for you. The dog must know about your exits, and the preferred place in your garden.

The crossbred dog, the mongrel, can be charming and is very cheap to buy but no cheaper to maintain, to feed, to inoculate, or to house and board. The first cross between two pedigree dogs has no advantage over the definite mongrel; in fact the inter-

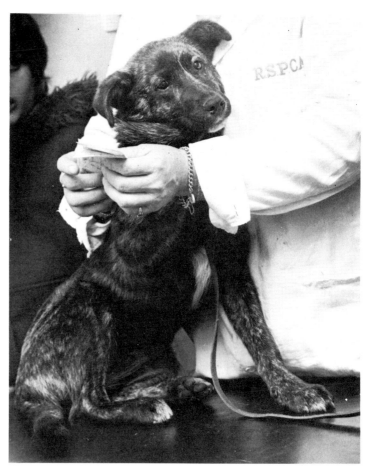

action of genes from two animals bred for dissimilar purposes can result in a very awkward dog indeed. I have in mind several boxer/Labrador crosses I have known which seemed to exhibit the worst traits of both breeds and the virtues of neither. The main disadvantage of the crossbreed is that its size, coat texture, and temperament are unpredictable. Mongrels do not have the eye-pleasing purity of form seen in a thorough-bred animal. It will usually also be true that the mongrel litter has not been reared with as much care and concern, as you might expect when you remember that the selling price is so low.

There is no statistical support for the commonly expressed theory that the mongrel is healthier and hardier than the purpose-bred, pedigree dog. It may well be that in a mongrel litter only the strongest survive, and they have an element of hybrid vigour, which may also bring with it an instinct for restless wandering. It is not true that you will avoid all the disadvantages of close relative breeding, as practised by the show breeds to fix type. One adventurous male can sire many puppies around his home, mating indiscriminately with his daughters and granddaughters in a far more concentrated way than a planned breeding programme would allow. If you buy a cross-bred puppy, get it wormed, de-flead, and inoculated just that much earlier than you would a pedigree puppy from a reliable source. Take even more care to keep it within your boundaries, because the wandering instinct which begot it may well be present in the offspring.

The border collie, recently recognized by The Kennel Club for beauty shows, has a breed register and pedigree system of its own. Border collies excel at obedience training because they have been bred to work to man's orders for many generations as cattle- and sheep-herding dogs. Without having some form of work border collies may become neurotic. The dogs I refer to as 'typed' for want of a better word, include the hunt terriers, Jack Russell terriers, lurchers, Lucas terriers, Webster terriers, and other strains which enthusiasts are trying to stabilize so that they may receive Kennel Club recognition. Foxhounds have their own pedigrees, but are not recognized by The Kennel Club. The little terriers are gay, happy personalities, displaying the pedigree terrier characteristics without breeding true to type consistently. Lurchers are delightful, gentle characters, having some greyhound or whippet in their make up. They are very fast, determined hunters. Sporting papers are the best source for puppies of these typed dogs that really need some work to keep them happy. Hunt terriers, lurchers, and foxhounds all have their own specialist shows in Britain, run by the breeds' own particular authorities, out-

Above It is very un-
desirable that dogs
should be allowed to
use the same crockery
as humans, as this
basenji is doing.
Left Barkless basenji
from the Sudan.
Right Foxhounds of the
Eridge Hunt under the
control of the whipper-
in.

side The Kennel Club's jurisdiction.

Pedigree dogs are those animals which breed true to type, with known parentage recorded for at least three generations, and of a breed recognized by a kennel club. Pedigree dogs may or may not be kennel club registered, but if you mean to show your dog then it must be registered. Most keen breeders register all their stock at birth with an identifying kennel name, although with increasing fees some may only register the most promising puppies. In Britain it is possible for the breeder to have a registration endorsed *Not eligible for exhibition, Progeny not eligible for registration*, or *Not eligible for issue of an export pedigree*. The first two endorsements will be used for dogs which are substandard in some way, and the last because the breeder wishes the stock to remain within the United Kingdom. These endorsements must stand unless rescinded by the person who made them, so that it will be as well to make sure that your puppy's registration does not conflict with your plans.

A puppy bought unregistered may be registered by the new owner, but it costs more than if the breeder had done so. If unregistered dogs are used for breeding, then their puppies are also more expensive to register, because without registration, there is no check that a pedigree is authentic. As regulations in Britain now stand, it is not possible to check that the pedigree belongs to the individual puppy that you are buying. If the puppy is registered, The Kennel Club will check for you that this puppy is possible. That is, its ancestors are of the breed stated, and the champions claimed are indeed true. Deaths of registered dogs are not recorded at The Kennel Club, so that it is not even possible to check that the sire and dam were alive at the time of the mating. In some countries, Germany, for example, regulations are very strict and all puppies in a litter must be registered at birth, and until the recent 'Eurovet' congress when the rule was rescinded only six were allowed to be reared. British dog breeding is founded upon good faith and integrity, and there is very little abuse of the pedigree system. In Britain, puppies are registered within four months of birth but there is no real proof that they were part of the litter claimed. So many pedigree puppies are being registered now that documentation is becoming unwieldy, and the Kennel Club has set up a two-tier registration system to separate the pedigree companion dog from those intended for breeding and exhibition.

If you are intending to buy a dog to show, then it is as well to declare your intention, so that the breeder can direct you to puppies with the acceptable markings and conformation. Such stock will be priced higher than those puppies which are sound but not show quality, that is, puppies suitable for companion status which make up the bulk of every litter. A 'show' puppy is no more than a puppy which looks likely to conform to accepted show standard. It cannot be shown until it is six months old, and so much can alter in that time, particularly in head formation when the second teeth come through at about four or five months. If picking a show puppy was not a mixture of instinct and gambling, much of the interest would be taken from dog showing. Sometimes it is possible to buy a dog that has already had some successes. Such an animal will be expensive, and may not continue to win if it does not take the change of ownership happily, or if your presentation is not as good as the first owner.

As a generalization, show classes for males are less full than for bitches, making competition easier. The reasoning behind this is that if a bitch fails to win, or does not make the best of herself in the show ring, she can always be mated to a good male and may produce something better. A male that fails to win has no future beyond becoming a companion dog, and if showing is the primary interest, then the owner must get another animal to exhibit. Much of the zest goes out of attending shows if you cannot take part in the competition.

CHOICE OF BREEDS

The Kennel Club classifies dogs into two divisions: **sporting** and **non-sporting**. The sporting dogs are further divided into *hound group, terriers*, and *gundogs*, and the non-sporting into *working dogs, toy dogs*, and *utility dogs*.

THE HOUND GROUP

It is as difficult to make generalizations about the dog groups as it is to pronounce on the characteristics of human nationalities; but it is fair to say that the hounds are mostly of very ancient, prehistoric lineage, proud and beautiful, independent and self-willed. The hunting instinct is so in-bred that you cannot hope to eradicate it; your hound will always hunt if given the chance, and will not always respond to your call when it is after a quarry. It is only comparatively recently that some of these pack dogs have been kept as domestic pets, and they are not the quickest to pick up the idea of house-training, nor are they easily confined within fences. They all need the chance to stretch their legs to the full at free exercise. The Kennel Club hound group comprises the Asian Afghans and salukis, the Russian borzoi, the very old breed of the German dachshund which comes in two sizes and three different coat types, the Mediterranean Ibizan and pharaoh hounds, the Scandinavian elkhounds and Finnish spitz, the African basenji and Rhodesian ridge-back, the basset hound which was developed in France, the Scottish deerhound, the Irish wolfhound, and the traditionally British beagle, bloodhound, greyhound, and whippet. The British foxhound, kept in hunt packs, is not eligible for Kennel Club registration.

The Afghan in show coat is a creature of great beauty, but takes a great deal of work to keep that way. A pet Afghan would probably have a lot of its fringes shortened to make it easier to keep clean. It is not an easy dog to train, and very difficult to stop once it gets into its stride at free exercise. The Afghan and its cousin the saluki were bred from the earliest times of civilization in Egypt to accompany horsemen over great distances in the desert. Both saluki and Afghan hunt by sight; they are aloof with strangers and sometimes a little fey, seeing and fearing things that others cannot see.

The borzoi is built on the lines of the greyhound, but has a long, silky coat. It is a composed, self-contained dog of great dignity, not really suited to the bustle of the average household.

The dachshund was originally bred to hunt both above and below ground. Very few now work as packs, but as individuals they have become very popular pets. They are obstinate and destructive if left alone, and noisy because when working the deep bay-bark was an asset in locating the dog and its quarry. They are also cheerful, courageous, and energetic. The standard should weigh up to 25 pounds (11 kilograms), the miniature less than half that weight. The smooth coat polishes like antique furniture, the long-haired type is silky with attractive fringes, and the wire-haired is covered in a grizzle-tweed, harsh coat which needs some preparation for showing. The miniature dogs were developed to go to ground after rabbits. The smooth dachshund has in common with other very short-coated breeds a tendency to skin troubles. All dachshunds with an exaggerated length of back are candidates for spinal weakness.

The Ibizan and pharaoh hounds are extremely lithe and elegant. Their appearance has changed little since they were depicted in the tombs and the temples of Ancient Egypt. They are long-distance sprinters and high jumpers; and to keep them in conditions with an excess of noise is cruel. Their high-pricked ears give them very acute hearing. They are not dogs for towns and noisy families.

Elkhounds from Norway and the Finnish spitz are similar in outline, having erect ears, plumed tails curled over the back, and deep, weather-proofed coats. The elkhound is greyish black, the 'Finkie' a deep, fox red. These are dogs that love activity in the open air, not boredom in overheated homes.

Basenjis, used as hunting dogs by the natives of the Sudan and Zaire, are often termed barkless dogs but they yodel/howl instead. Like all hounds they are independent, and keen hunters.

The Rhodesian ridgeback is a big dog, weighing about 80 pounds (36 kilograms) guaranteed to frighten off the ill-intentioned intruder. They were used by Boer farmers to hunt big game, hence the nickname, the lion dog. It is very pleasant and cheerful in the home, and is lion coloured with the distinctive ridge of reversed hair from the nape of the neck the whole length of the spine. In a show specimen the ridge should end in two identical whorls. Ridgebacks are affected by a congenital abnormality of ingrowing skin, known as dermoid cysts, which must be removed surgically.

The basset hound has only become popular as a pet in the last decade; before that it was strictly a pack hound to hunt hare. Its woebegone appearance, pendulous ears, and inward-crooked forelegs have appealed to the public, and it has become very sought

Above A Münsterlander enjoying a swim.
Left Play between dogs simulates fight action.
Right A dog can be taught to be trust-worthy with creatures which would be its normal prey.

after as a pet. It is really a big dog on short legs, and needs plenty of work and hard exercise.

The Celtic pair, the Irish wolfhound and the Scottish deerhound are giant dogs, topping 120 pounds (54 kilograms), with rough, wiry coats. These are not pack dogs and need human company, and exercise over rough ground. They are magnificent animals, gentle and faithful, but it would be cruel to acquire one as a status symbol for suburban conditions.

The beagle is another hound only lately come to pet status. They were originally pack hounds kept for hare and weasel hunting. Medium sized, short coated, good tempered, and tolerant of other dogs, they appear to be the ideal in family pets, except that generations of kennel living makes them somewhat slow to house-train, and if they can get out of your garden, they will. The beagle is also the favoured dog of research establishments, because it is so easy to deal with, and not a fussy feeder; in fact, it thrives on nutritional trials, and tests out the new lines in dog food for its fellow canines with enthusiasm.

The bloodhound is a very big and powerful dog, a specialist's animal. Following a scent and tracking is its job and it should be employed, or have stimulating exercise devised for it. Bloodhounds need careful feeding and observation afterwards, because the breed is subject to bloat, (stomach distention and torsion) needing help at once, day or night. A bloodhound is definitely not a dog to buy without careful study of the breed.

The greyhound and its smaller cousin the whippet are elegant, gentle, devoted creatures. They must have periods of free, fast exercise, but when indoors they are very restful companions, with trouble-free, smooth coats. Ex-racing greyhounds are sometimes offered for sale, looking for second homes, when they are quite young. They make very agreeable pets, but you will have to house-train them, and make sure your neighbour's cat does not invade the garden.

When considering a hound breed, remember that they are all frustrated workers. They must have good free exercise and firm handling.

THE TERRIER GROUP

Terriers are tough, bold, hardy, and courageous, used to more kicks than dinners in former times. They were bred to hunt and kill predators and vermin. The terrier is quick moving and vocal, essentially active, and not slow to defend its honour in a fight with its own kind. Digging is one of its hereditary skills, and do not be surprised if it turns its attention to getting moles out of your flower border, if no other game is available. There is a large number of regional varieties of terrier, varying in size and coat colour: Airedales – the largest terrier; cairns; dandie dinmonts; Irish; Welsh; Lakeland; Kerry blue; Scottish and Skye; Norfolk and Norwich; and West Highland whites; as well as smooth- or wire-coated fox terriers, and the Sealyhams.

All these terriers' coats need expert trimming for show presentation, and if showing is the intention, the puppy coat must be stripped in the correct way from the beginning. Many show terriers are placed in the charge of professional handlers who will have care of the dog, performing the trimming and exhibiting for the owner. It is quite useless to enter an unprepared terrier pet in the show ring. The border terrier is an exception, because it is shown in its natural state. The Bedlington has a different type of coat, but one that needs a great deal of work to get into show trim. It is inclined to look shaggy unless given regular attention.

Bull terriers and Staffordshire bull terriers were bred as fighting dogs, and old time meat tenderizers; they were employed to tantalize a tethered bull just before he was killed, because it was thought this made the meat better for eating. These dogs are charming at home, but their inbred courage makes them strong willed, needing a dominant owner, or they will be a liability to take out in public. Given the chance, they relish a fight; they are heavyweight for their size, packed full of muscle and ready to meet trouble half way. White bull terriers run the risk of being congenitally deaf, a condition recognizable at about six weeks old when the puppy does not respond to a clanging food dish. A deaf puppy must be put down, it has absolutely no future. It is a mistaken kindness to try to keep it in these days of machinery and motorized vehicles.

THE GUNDOG GROUP

The gundog is bred as a companion to the shooting man, to flush out game, to indicate where it has fallen, or to retrieve it. Smart shoots employ spaniels to go through cover and flush game, and retrievers to bring back the birds. The rough shooter will have an all-purpose dog which will attempt all the different duties. Gundogs which have won competitions for shooting attributes will be aspiring to qualification as field champions, those which have won both at beauty shows and in the field have dual qualifications. Gundogs are docile, easily managed, and gentle mouthed, making themselves very agreeable pets for the household that never intends to go shooting. In the show ring, all gundogs must have the level bite and soft mouth necessary for carrying game without mangling it. Steadiness is essential in the working gundog, and it would be a great pity if this attribute was lost by over-breeding purely for pets. Gundog breeds must not be shy, jumpy, and irritable. They must also be tolerant of the presence of other dogs, and not jealous.

The English, Gordon, and Irish setters have to some extent lost their original purpose, which was to creep low through cover, driving the game into nets. Now that it is the custom to shoot birds on the wing, the setter has adapted to be an all-purpose gundog. The English setter is white with lemon, blue, or liver flecks, the Gordon black, trimmed with tan, the Irish (red) setter is a glorious bronze red. These are tall, amiable dogs, full of fun, and playful as puppies, with tails that may easily sweep all the ornaments off your tables; they need to be conditioned early to good behaviour indoors.

The British pointer and the German short-haired pointer will point, hunt, and retrieve. They are active and hardy, and must have plenty of exercise or work to prevent them becoming soft.

The Labrador retriever is one of Britain's most popular dogs, it is widely used as a guide dog for the blind, and a detector dog for the police and customs officials. The yellow variety, which is now almost more popular than the black, may vary from pale cream to golden, but it is not correct to refer to a 'golden' Labrador. Chocolate remains an interesting minority colour. The Labrador is easy to feed, hardy, and produces litters easily of as many as ten or fourteen puppies at a time. All these factors have tended to contribute to indiscriminate over-breeding, because Labradors of a kind are very easy to breed indeed. The Labrador suffers from congenital eye diseases, and a degeneration of the hip joint, known as hip dysplasia (HD). This particular disease is found in all breeds, but some are more generally affected than others. In an effort to breed away from defects the original equable and easy temperament of the Labrador is in danger of being lost; lack of work and purpose may be a contributory factor. When buying a Labrador puppy it is as well to inquire if the parents' hips and eyes have been examined, and what the verdict was. Dogs with perfect hips may throw affected puppies, and the breeder must not be blamed, unless they are breeding from a position of ignorance of the condition of their dog. Hip dysplasia is seldom so bad as to cripple the puppy. The dog may go through a phase of lameness in youth, however, and then the joint will produce compensating bone so that the animal can move with ease, showing no trace of disability, until arthritis may set into the joint in old age. Labradors are greedy, and easily made slack and soft bodied through over-feeding and under-exercising. They require regular walks and well-fenced gardens for their noses take them far afield.

The Weimaraner was a very exclusive German gundog, which was not widely exported until after World War II. The distinctive silvery grey, 'milk chocolate by moonlight' colour is unforgettable, earning Weimaraners the nickname of 'grey ghosts'. The eyes are a piercing yellow/hazel, imparting a less kindly expression than found in most gundogs. Weimaraners are inveterate hunters, and can take hard exercise – if conditions are safe, they enjoy a trot beside a ridden bicycle. This dog trains well and is used as a police dog, but it is not a gregarious animal, being more attached to one owner than to a family.

Cocker spaniels are perennial favourites. They are probably a very ancient variety of English spaniel although it was not until the end of the 1800s that it was recognized by The Kennel Club. Glamorous and hardy, cocker spaniels fulfil for many people the rôle of the ideal pet. Their coats and particularly their ears must be kept clean and tidy. Hereditary eye conditions, HD, and temperament of parents warrant inquiry when buying.

This Afghan hound is in full show coat which needs a great deal of grooming care.

The Pharaoh hound with its wide-open ears is very sensitive to sound.

Salukis were developed to hunt jackal and gazelle.

A Rhodesian ridgeback showing the characteristic ridge of reversed hair down its spine.

English and Welsh springer spaniels are larger dogs, with less feathering (fringes of hair) than the cocker. They make excellent pets but should have constructive play and exercise or work to make their lives happy.

The golden retriever is a very popular dog, a big, amiable teddy bear with a flat or wavy golden coat which should never be curly. It has a charming nature and it is very intelligent. Ethical breeders of goldens are trying hard to eradicate hereditary diseases which bedevil this lovely breed. You should always ask about the amount of veterinary examination the parents have had. You may not find parents with perfect hips, but there are many dogs which have passed the examinations for hereditary cataract and progressive retinal atrophy. Satisfy yourself that the breeder is acting on a basis of knowledge. Most of the gundogs have a long life, spaniels quite often reaching fourteen years of age.

THE WORKING GROUP

These dogs are still thought to have a job in life, although many thousands are kept in the home as pets, combining a life of leisure with guarding duties. The Alsatian, which is more properly known as the German shepherd dog, is a very popular breed. It is used in many countries as a police and army dog, as a guide for the blind, crowd controller and farm dog. Not a dog to make friends lightly, the German shepherd dog is devoted to its own family. If you make this dog your pride you will have a particularly fine animal and need fear no violence when it is by your side. To encourage this breed to do 'man work', that is, to attack people is extremely dangerous and is not to be encouraged for the average owner. Do see both parents of a litter, and be careful to note the surroundings in which they are raised. German shepherd dogs have large litters, and early damage may be done if the puppies are not well kept with sufficient space and food from early days.

The boxer breed is only 100 years old. It is the clown of the guard dogs. It is ready to play, even into old age, but it takes guard work very seriously. The dogs can be very boisterous in youth, and most make a bid for domination at about a year old when they will be deliberately disobedient to see how far you will let them go. Boxers delight in rough play, but they adjust well to babies and tiny children. Boxer breeders have improved the head of the animal markedly, and the breed does not generally suffer from breathing troubles, but there is some hereditary epilepsy and heart disease. Stud dogs should have been tested for these conditions. The boxer faints easily owing to its head construction, but soon recovers if ice or wet cloths are put on the head and neck. The boxer is particularly dependent on human company, and has a reputation for being destructive if left alone long, but is probably not actually worse than other breeds. The boxer's powerful shoulders and jaws make it an excellent demolition worker. Boxer bitches are very easy to handle and loving. They are smaller than the males and more obedient and anxious to please their owner. White, or white with coloured patches are unacceptable colours, and these puppies may be congenitally stone deaf.

The Dobermann pinscher is another working police and army dog. It is tall and elegant in black-and-tan, brown-and-tan, and blue-and-tan. Dobermanns were bred as guard dogs by the German, Louis Dobermann, and probably include pinscher, German pointer, Rottweiler, Manchester terrier and greyhound blood. They are very brave, and can be fierce with strangers. They must always have firm handling.

The bull mastiff is one of the larger guarding breeds, males weighing up to 130 pounds (58·5 kilograms). They are very even tempered, and not so boisterous as the smaller guard breeds.

Great Danes are lordly and have always held their appeal for those who like a large, agile, powerful dog. A dog should be at least 32 inches (80 centimetres) at the withers. They are not easy to raise as puppies, needing careful regulation of food and exercise to achieve their size and heavy bone on straight legs. Danes are usually friendly, affectionate, and intelligent.

The Rottweiler is a dog of great intelligence which must be sensibly owned to get the best of its many virtues. It is very handsome in black with light brown and mahogany markings.

All these guarding breeds are potential challengers for domination within the family. The dog will try to become pack leader, taking orders from no one, refusing to obey unless it suits it. This is an intolerable situation with any dog, but is potentially extremely dangerous with a large one. These breeds must be kindly but firmly treated from puppy days. Every command given must be carried out, and every attempt at defiance quelled, without breaking the dog's spirit by making it lose its self-respect.

Manoeuvre sometimes as you would with a child, providing distraction, or putting the dog in a situation where it wants to obey. Obedience must become a habit rather than a battle to be fought out every day.

The sled-pulling dogs of the far North, Samoyeds, huskies, and Alaskan Malamutes are used to co-operating with man to some extent, but they exhibit some inter-pack jealousy. These are not dogs for your first trial in pet ownership.

The many varieties of herding dogs are much easier to manage. Their ability to round up sheep, cattle, or poultry can be used to advantage for obedience competition work. Perhaps the best known is the rough collie, and the smaller relation, the Shetland sheepdog, fondly known as the Sheltie. The smooth collie with all the same attributes other than coat, is less glamorous but requires less grooming.

Bearded collies with their long, harsh, flat topcoat and soft, dense undercoat are not difficult to groom, and need no trimming.

The Old English sheepdog, or bobtail as it is sometimes called, is another matter altogether. Extreme length and depth of coat is desirable, and the show dog condition is not easy to maintain. Old English sheepdog combings may be spun like wool, but they are not appreciated over furniture. This is not a breed to buy because you fell in love with a picture of one, because in practice you will not want to keep it in long coat. A breed created for cold outdoor conditions, the bobtail is not happy in over-heated rooms. Nevertheless, the attractive appearance of this dog has made it very popular, and as a result the temperament is now questionable. Make sure you can offer this dog a life suited to its needs.

Briards from France, and Hungarian pulis are among the continental sheep-herding dogs now being bred in Britain. The puli's long corded coat is easy to care for, if you enjoy hairdressing. You can sit on the floor with a puli and divide up its cords endlessly; if this is not done the puli could become smelly and matted.

The popular little Welsh corgis are cattle dogs. The Pembroke is the better known dog. The Cardigan has a long, natural tail and attractive colours in the coat, any but white being allowed in the show ring.

The Pyrenean mountain dog and the Saint Bernard are giants of the sheep-herding dogs. In former times they were kept for guarding the flock rather than herding. At 125 pounds (56 kilograms) top weight for the Pyrenean and 200 pounds (90 kilograms) for the Saint Bernard they are as big or bigger than some people, a fact to be taken into consideration before you fall for the attractive, cuddly puppies.

THE TOY GROUP

Toy dogs are not silly, by any means. Many pack great verve and courage in a small frame. The Cavalier King Charles spaniel is deservedly popular; it is the largest of the toy dogs, and of particularly agreeable temperament. These happy little dogs deserve a daily grooming to prevent their fringes matting. While they are very good-tempered as family pets and town dogs, they become all-spaniel when working a hedgerow or putting up game. Show competition is keen. Their eyes should be large and lustrous; the tricolours must be well broken with white, the black-and-tan and the ruby varieties must show no white, and on the 'Blenheim' the red and white colouring should show the typical spot in the centre of the forehead. A very desirable show point is a level bite, that is, the top puppy teeth should just overlap the lower ones. An undershot dog (lower jaw protruding further than upper jaw) stands little chance in the show ring, and although many puppies are sold on the assurance that the bite will be level when the second teeth come through, this is by no means certain. What the exhibitor terms 'a bad mouth' just means uneven teeth placement; it does not affect the dog's eating ability, or its life as a pet. These little dogs are very easy to show, demanding no expertise, but the dogs must have an expression of gaiety and happiness.

The less common King Charles spaniel is smaller and has a shorter face than the Cavalier – the ancestors of the modern Cavalier were bred from the longest headed of the King Charles spaniels. The King Charles comes in the same four colours as the Cavalier, but is easily distinguished by the short foreface and the domed head. The

Cavalier makes the best pet for an active mixed age group family, but the King Charles spaniel suits a mature individual better.

The chihuahua which may be either long-, or smooth-coated, has a huge following of admirers. Its weight, averaging 4 pounds (1·8 kilograms) makes the chihuahua a possible pet for many people. Chihuahuas are very agile and seem to be able to avoid being stumbled over. It is a very game dog, conscious of its own dignity, and does not appreciate being mauled by strangers. The chihuahua is not the dog for a boisterous family.

For a dog weighing a maximum of 11 pounds (5 kilograms), the Pekingese is majestic, charming, but certainly obstinate. Regular daily grooming is essential. In cool weather, the Pekingese enjoys a country walk as well as any other dog.

The Pomeranian is another little dog that is not gregarious. It is a dainty little animal that does not require much formal exercise if it can enjoy the freedom of a medium sized garden.

The papillon is a tiny dog about chihuahua size, with huge butterfly ears from whence comes its name. Very gay and active it keeps busy in quite a small garden, as does the little monkey-faced griffon, obtainable in smooth or rough coat.

The pug is heavier, with a smoother coat, and a warm, comforting snore when asleep.

By far the most popular toy at the moment is the Yorkshire terrier. It is a game, hardy little terrier but it would be impossible to keep the family pet in the length of coat desirable for a show dog.

English toy terriers (black-and-tan), miniature pinschers, and Italian greyhounds are all small versions of the big breeds, with much the same characteristics of the large counterparts. As a generalization the smaller versions are noisier and more restless.

THE UTILITY GROUP

All the dogs which do not fit into the other categories are included in this group.

The poodles are the most popular; the standard poodle is a big dog measuring up to 22 inches (55 centimetres at the withers), the miniature is 11 to 15 inches (28 to 38 centimetres), and the toys under 11 inches (28 centimetres). The lion clip, in which you see the show dogs looking so glamorous, is not practical to maintain for the pet dog. Once again, do not buy because of an attractive dog in a picture, but buy for the fun and intelligence of this breed. These are sensitive dogs, anxious to be in tune with their owner's wishes, more suitable for adults than noisy families. Be very particular about the soundness of the parents when you buy. Many coat colours are available, but those broken with white cannot be shown.

Chow chows are dogs you tend to like if you know. They are proud, even haughty with strangers, and do not give their friendship lightly.

The bulldog has a wonderful temperament. This is another big dog on shortish legs. It was bred for determination and the bulldog has it still. It suffers in hot weather and stressful conditions from swelling of the soft palate at the back of the throat. Most owners find it useful to have a vacuum flask of ice with them in hot weather to cool the dog down. In common with all the short-faced breeds they are not popular passengers in aircraft flying at high altitudes.

Bostons and French bulldogs are both gallant and gay little dogs with bulldog blood. Both make loving pets, but they should not be whelped by a novice without expert help to hand, because in common with other large-headed breeds with small waists, they have their whelping problems. As you might expect the puppies are usually more expensive than easier whelping breeds.

Dalmatians need plenty of regular exercise and demand human company. The hereditary malady is a tendency for stones to form obstructing the urinary system.

The shih tzu is increasing in popularity rapidly. It is an intelligent dog and makes a good companion especially if you enjoy grooming because it needs daily attention and a tidy up after meals. All the Tibetan breeds are becoming fashionable, including the lhasa apsos, the Tibetan spaniels and terriers. They all have a reserved manner with strangers; they are active and can do as much or as little as you want from them.

There are many recognized breeds, not numerically very strong, but with ardent admirers, which have not been mentioned. Many generalizations have been made which will not apply to every individual in a breed, and there are no two dogs exactly alike. The character will be different even if the markings are just the same.

Dog care

The most important thing in life to the pet dog is companionship. A dog may *exist* on poor food, with a dirty coat, and in harsh conditions but it will be devoted to the owner who shares the same standard of living, as long as they are together. A dog left alone too long will indicate by barking or by being destructive that it is miserably lonely. A young puppy must be conditioned to staying alone for periods up to one hour after it has been fed and exercised. It is unreasonable, however, to expect the large active breeds to be confined in a small kitchen for several hours, especially when there are likely to be callers who will alert them and make them feel frustrated at not being able to see who is at the door. You should not consider owning a dog if you know you will be leaving it alone for several hours every day only to bring it into full use at weekends, as a family amenity.

The puppy that is talked to, has its needs anticipated, and mistakes curbed at once is the one quickly and easily trained, the dog that is a pleasure to own. Puppies take time and need constant attention. An older dog already in the household may take on a good deal of the tuition and supply the necessary company for a puppy, but two animals are likely to be more devoted to each other than each individual would be to its owner.

The dog that is going to share your life will need to become accustomed to many situations which may cause stress unless it has encountered them early on. The animal that has complete confidence in its owner, however, will usually become conditioned to playing a supporting rôle to human companions no matter where their interests may take it.

CAR TRAVEL

If you are a car owner you will want to accustom your dog to travel with you, and indeed its very first journey may be when you collect it from the kennels. The puppy should make this traumatic trip held in your arms, so that it feels secure. To minimize the chance of travel sickness it will probably not have been fed. Many puppies do drool and vomit in the car at first, but they should outgrow the tendency. I think it better to continue taking the dog out (naturally before feeding) and be ready to cope with vomiting, rather than resort to tranquillizers or other drugs. The puppy must be taught from the start that it is supposed to sit or lie where you wish in the car, and that it does not leap about or play. It is an admission of failure to have to tie a dog down in a car, and it is also dangerous. Seat belts for dogs can be bought, and have their uses if the dog has to travel with a small child on the back seat. The large dog is best suited by an estate car with a separate wired compartment at the back where it may lie at full stretch instead of constantly slipping off the passenger seat. Wire mesh window panels are available to ensure ventilation in summer at the same time preventing the dog putting its head out of the open window, a practice with dangers for the dog and other road users. Even with full ventilation, a car heats up very quickly in summer when it is parked, and dogs need more air than do people. Great attention must be paid to the length of time the dog is left in the car, or you may return to find it distressed or even unconscious.

RAIL TRAVEL

Most dogs travel well by train in the passenger compartment. Take a rug to cover the seat or teach your dog to lie on the floor. Dogs may be sent by rail unaccompanied, when they will travel in the guard's van in a crate. Great care and organization is necessary to ensure that there will be no undue delays, especially if there is a break in the journey. Unaccompanied train travel is not to be recommended, however, especially for young puppies. It is most undesirable to have a new puppy sent to you by rail – the terrifying experience could affect its temperament for the rest of its life.

AIR TRAVEL

Dogs which are to travel by air must be crated in accordance with the regulations of the International Air Travel Act, or they may be refused at the airport. The box must be the height of the dog in standing position, twice the width of the dog across the shoulders, and of equal length to the dog measured from nose to root of tail plus an allowance equal to the distance from the ground to elbow joint. The box must fit the dog accurately, and should not be so large that the dog is buffeted. There must be through ventilation from top to bottom at both ends, and the sides should also have ventilation, at a level which can reach the dog when it is lying down. This is most important, because dogs have suffocated even when there are plenty of air inlets above them. The box must be strong enough for the breed, and reinforced against chewing on a long journey.

Space must be booked ahead for live freight, to ensure that if the aircraft flies the dog must be carried. A few airlines will carry crated dogs in the passenger cabin, by permission of the captain of the aircraft. In fact, dogs are happier in the semi-darkness of the freight hold, where they are undisturbed and may sleep the journey away. Dogs cannot fly in the passenger cabin coming into Britain, owing to the rabies laws, and no dog can ever fly uncrated. Some airlines are refusing to fly the short-nosed breeds, such as boxers, pekingese, pugs, and griffons when they travel at altitudes of 5000 to 8000 feet (1500 to 2400 metres), and some airlines will not fly live cargo at all. Veterinary surgeons advise against tranquillizing dogs before air travel, because the individual reaction varies so much. If the dog awakens from sedation into a frightening situation it may become hysterical.

WATER

Many dogs like to swim. Some will dive in from a boat or jetty, but the majority prefer to wade in. Swimming comes naturally to a

Travelling in the back of an estate car in a collapsible bed with wire guard to prevent interference with other occupants.

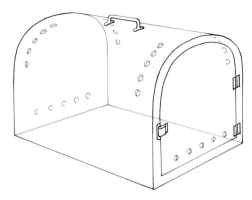

This transparent plastic box is convenient for conveying small dogs safely for short periods, but is unsuitable for air travel.

Dogs will not be accepted by airlines unless in a correctly sized and proportioned air travel box, to conform with International Air Traffic Regulations (1 October 1974).

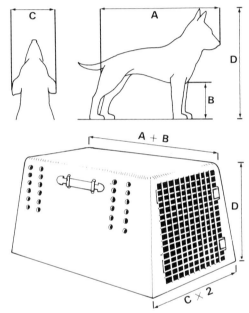

It is dangerous to allow your dog off the lead on a cliff walk, because if it puts up a fox, rabbit, or gull it could easily go over the edge. The dog cannot anticipate danger of this type. On cliffs and downland the adder flourishes in high summer, and may strike if nosed out by the dog. If this should happen carry the dog to the nearest veterinary surgeon at once for treatment. You will see that the affected area will immediately swell and you will not wish to accelerate the spread of the poison through the body by exercise.

COUNTRYSIDE

The penalties for chasing any farm livestock are extremely severe, and the farmer also has the law on his side if he shoots at any dog caught chasing, or showing intention of chasing, or even on the scene where livestock has been injured. Apart from always looking two fields ahead to make sure that your dog does not get into a compromising situation, it is essential to invest in third party insurance cover against any damage that your dog may do. Many breed clubs include this cover in their subscription, or it is possible to extend your household policy to cover damage done by the dog, from tripping up an old lady with its lead, to knocking a man off a bike. None of these incidents is easy on the owner, and it is much better to avoid accidents by having good control of your dog. When you and your dog are in the country you should also be on the lookout for fields being sprayed with pesticides or herbicides which might easily upset or even fatally poison your pet. The dog does not have to eat a poisonous substance in the fields – it can lick an effective quantity from its paws when cleaning them.

dog, but it may tire, or swim out too far after a toy, so you should always watch out for it. After your dog has been swimming in salt water its coat should be rinsed free of salt which can otherwise irritate the skin. On beaches there are often the decomposing remains of seabirds or picnic leftovers which will be eaten with relish only to be vomited up again soon after. Eating an oiled seabird has been known to cause severe poisoning in the dog. Most dogs have to learn from experience that salt water is not for drinking; a bout of vomiting and diarrhoea will follow. If you take your dog when you go for a picnic on the beach provide some shade for it to lie in, and take a bottle of fresh water, or a few icecubes in a vacuum container, to provide the dog with a cool drink.

One of the great pleasures of owning a dog is in observing its behaviour pattern, its character, and its intelligence. These features vary within their breeds just as much as human beings' do. No two dogs, even from the same litter and brought up together, are exactly alike. A dog that lives close to its owner develops its potential intelligence and canine characteristics, as well as becoming what we term 'clever'. It learns to appreciate and understand its owner's mood, and adjust its behaviour accordingly. To watch your dog's approach to varying stimuli is fascinating. The young dog needs about the same amount of supervision as you would give a child of about three years of age.

URBAN CONTROL

In towns your dog should wear a leather collar and separate lead, with a strong hook in good repair. The lead should be kept short and the dog close by your side. Many shops bar dogs, but it should be tied securely if it is left outside, no matter how obedient you consider your dog to be, because there will always be some factor capable of breaking a dog's concentration. People can be extremely thoughtless in trying to attract the dog obviously left to sit, and few dogs are trained to the standard that will make them undisturbed by temptation; probably only police and army dogs reach this stage of absolute obedience.

Some towns have bye-laws which impose fines on the owners of dogs which foul the pavements. I do not favour training a dog to use the gutter to defecate, however. Too many have been injured or killed by cars which came in too close; roads are too crowded to allow any margin for error. The simplest way is to encourage the use of your own garden. Guide dogs for the blind are taught always to use the garden, because of the problems which would arise if the animal were to stop when on duty. Take the dog to an open space where it will not offend anyone. There are various devices available on the scoop and plastic bag principal which a town-dwelling owner may use to remove offending excrement. It is antisocial behaviour to walk your dog round a built-up area to defecate outside other people's gates, or worse still, in open-plan gardens. It is quite unnecessary to take a bitch in season into public places at all; she will not deteriorate through having little exercise for three weeks, and you and other dog owners will be spared embarrassment and trouble. The odour of a bitch in season is a trigger to so much compulsive behaviour by the male dog that responsible owners will not let them off the lead but if the bitches are also closely confined there is less tantalization. The mating urge is not one sided, and the bitch will, at the fertile period mid-heat, be just as anxious to meet the dog, and very strict vigilance is needed, including accompanying her to the garden, and closing ground-floor windows at night. Bitches become particularly tense just before coming into season, and may be more destructive, disobedient, or noisy at this time. Two bitches kept together may become irritable and fight. You should keep a check on the date, and carefully observe the behaviour of the bitch so that you know when the season is due.

Dogs do respond to stress situations in the family, or even to the absence of one person overnight. Dependent pet animals are quite capable of producing psychosomatic illness, ceasing to eat and displaying inertia and depression in a situation that does not please them. The interest you take in your pet will help you to diagnose the reasons for alteration in its behaviour which are not caused by direct physical illness.

NUTRITION

Correct metabolism provided by balanced feeding provides a glow to the coat, a shine to the eyes, alert carriage, and a happy demeanour that cannot be achieved in any other way. Good feeding for the dog is not necessarily expensive feeding, certainly not extravagant use of costly protein. Many overfed dogs are seen in veterinary surgeries. The dog's meal times are a very important part of its day, and it should be fed, if possible at a separate time from its owner so that full attention may be given to the pet. A delicate puppy can be ruined if fed too little, too much, or overdosed with vitamin and mineral supplements and conditioners. In particular the excess use of codliver oil (vitamin D) may result in bone malformation and completely cripple a dog. Some veterinary surgeons specializing in orthopaedics have declared that they have seen more cases of bone dystrophies through over dosage with codliver or halibutliver oil than they have seen dogs with rickets caused by deprivation. Dogs do not need conditioning powders but they do require a diet designed for their intestinal system, and veterinary advice if they are ill. No all-purpose conditioner can hope to reverse disease, and the healthy dog is its own conditioner anyway.

Like man and other mammals, the dog needs a balanced diet of protein, carbohydrates, fat, vitamins, minerals, and water. It is quite wrong to think that because the dog is termed a carnivore it should eat solely meat. An experimental trial of feeding dogs only fine beef steak caused their condition to deteriorate badly after only three weeks, and they would have died if kept on this diet longer. Overfeeding with meat puts a great strain on the kidneys. The dog must have an equal amount of carbohydrate in the form of biscuits, dog meal, or brown bread. Pet dogs need only 24 per cent of their food intake to be protein, and this need not be always in the form of meat – it may be varied by fish, cheese and cooked eggs, soya bean meal, or the new artificially manufactured proteins. The really hardworking farm or police dog, the bitch in whelp, or a dog kept in extremely cold conditions may need a little more protein.

Most people are used to assessing their own diets in terms of calories. The average woman needs about 2000 calories a day for maintenance, or if she is actively slimming 1000 calories a day are sufficient. The pet dog's calorie requirements may also be worked out, taking into account age, size, and activity. A growing puppy may need 100 calories a day for every pound of body weight (220 calories for each kilogram), while a lethargic old dog will only utilize about 25 calories per pound (55 cal/kg) of its weight. A tiny, toy adult dog, weighing 6 pounds (2·7 kg) will need less than 300 calories a day in food, the 25 pound (11·25 kg) Cavalier about 800 calories, the boxer at 70 pounds (31·5 kg) needs 1600 calories and the Great Dane weighing 140 pounds (53 kg) needs 2800 calories, which would be a generous allowance for a human of the same weight. The dog, of course, is more active than most humans and uses more energy. Dog biscuit gives about 1600 calories to the pound (3550 cal/kg), tinned dog meat 500 calories a pound (1100 cal/kg), and raw minced beef, as sold for hamburger, between 1100 and 1200 calories (2400 to 2650 cal/kg) depending on the water and fat content.

Dogs may be fed in many different ways, and a splendid animal can result from any of them. The pitfalls lie in mixing the ways, the diets and additives, and in thinking that because a little is good, more must be better. The traditional way to feed a dog was on household scraps and biscuits, but modern meal preparation leaves very little residual waste, certainly not in balanced proportions. While admitting that raw meat is the dog's favourite form of protein, we must take into account that there is a worldwide shortage and that price makes it impractical to feed to pets. Slaughterhouse meat, condemned meat, and offal are a health hazard to those handling it. If this meat is used preparation should be done somewhere other than the household kitchen, and knives and chopping boards should be sterilized after use.

In Britain, applicants for licences to breed from more than two bitches under the 1973 Breeding of Dogs Act are required to show that they have a separate refrigerator if they have to store slaughterhouse meat.

If meat is to be fed the formula is:

½ lb meat (preferably cooked)
½ lb biscuit meal or dried brown bread
1 teaspoonful sterilized bone flour
1 drop fresh codliver oil or other source of vitamin D

That is, 1 kg meat, 1 kg biscuit, 4 teaspoonful bone flour, 4 drops codliver oil, remembering that this makes a large quantity.

Sterilized bone flour is the best source of calcium, and must be used together with codliver oil for strong bones. Remember that overdosage of calcium and codliver oil can cause bone distortion. If ready-minced meat is bought, try to find out how much desiccated bone and fat is in it, and also that the meat is not sour, because the action of mincing heats it considerably. Ready minced meat which is then cooked may lose a lot of its calorie value due to the release of the fat content. Between 5 and 10 per cent of fat in the diet is desirable, and for dogs showing a scurfy skin or dry coat, or shedding hair excessively, more fat in the form of edible vegetable oil, margarine or suet may be added to the diet until the condition rights itself. The addition of fat makes food more palatable to the dog, and fussy feeders may respond to a little dripping-flavoured gravy poured over the meal.

The cheaper offals, tripe, lung melts, and heart may all be used for the protein element, but some breeds vary in their digestive capacity and may find heart too rich, and liver too laxative. Liver should never form more than·a small proportion of the meat offered; most dogs regard it as a very great treat but could reject other food in favour of it.

White fish, carefully boned, is a useful

alternative food, as are hardboiled eggs. Raw egg white can cause a vitamin deficiency producing hair loss, dermatitis, and poor growth. This is not to say that the dog will not appreciate licking up the egg you dropped on baking day, but raw eggs should not be fed consistently. Codliver oil should be bought in small quantity, because its vitamin value deteriorates in storage.

The biscuit meal should be a lightly baked, plain wheatmeal without meat or vitamin additives. Most dogs prefer the meal to be lightly soaked in water or gravy, and many breeders feel that to use soaked, small grade meal is one way to guard against stomach distention, bloat, and torsion to which the bigger breeds, particularly bloodhounds, are subject. Rapid, noticeable abdominal swelling soon after feeding needs veterinary attention fast, no matter what time of day. Only sufficient meal should be soaked for one feed at a time, because wet grain quickly turns sour. Brown or wholemeal bread is just as good and may be used as part or all of the dog's carbohydrate ration. Many dogs enjoy a hard biscuit after meals as tooth and jaw exercise and to fill up vacant corners. Other dogs thrive on a milk and cereal breakfast, particularly those that need building up, but an excess of milk can be laxative, especially in puppies.

The dog's stomach is able to expand a good deal, and most adults can take enough for one feeding every twenty-four hours, although less responsive dogs may appreciate the same ration broken down into two or even three meals. The time of day at which the adult is fed is not important but strenuous exercise and car journeys are better not taken immediately after a meal. Every dog's digestive system is different and it may be that your dog cannot eat something that all other dogs of your acquaintance thrive on. This is part of the interest of dog owning, but do be sure that it is the dog that cannot digest something and not your own prejudice that you are forcing on it.

It may be that instead of carefully measuring out the drop of codliver oil and the bone flour, you may wish to give one of the multiple additives on the market. Take veterinary advice on the best one to use, follow the dosage recommended for the weight of your dog, and do not give other vitaminized products, in addition.

The well-advertised brands of canned dog meat are excellent, and have a balanced measure of vitamins and minerals added to compensate for those lost during cooking. When using the best canned meats with wholemeal biscuit you need add nothing else at all. There are also available cans containing complete feeds, with cereal already added. They will seem to be lower priced but you will need more tins because you should not add extra bread or biscuit, or the ration will have too much starch. Much research has gone into the formulation of the best canned meats, and in particular great attention has been paid to palatability, so that the dog is eager to enjoy them. Unfortunately, some of these meats pass rather quickly through the intestine; there may be some dog-appeal left in the excreta, which the animal may reconsume, to the horror of the owner. *Coprophagy* is the technical term for this habit. There have been many explanations put forward for this not uncommon occurrence; it may be partly feral behaviour to remove traces of trail from the enemy, or partly parental instinct to consume puppy faeces; it may also be puppy experimentation at the stage when they will eat practically anything, or a possible pancreatic failure when food is being passed through the digestive system unprocessed. If the habit persists after a trial food change, veterinary advice must be sought.

The most modern method of feeding is to use a complete food based on soya bean protein, looking like a biscuit meal but lighter because it is expanded and air dried. These complete foods need nothing but water in addition, although owners may like to add a very small quantity of gravy, meat juices, or milk to vary flavour and keep up the dog's interest in eating. Some dogs will always eat what they are given; others are fussy and want tempting. Many puppies are weaned on to these air-dried, expanded meals and will then go through life happily on them, so that the dog's diet is trouble-free, clean and easy to handle, and has no need of refrigeration. There is the added bonus of being able to use assorted household scraps to accompany the already complete basic nourishment.

All dogs need constant access to fresh water; a springer spaniel, for example, needs about two pints (a little over a litre) every day but dogs on air-dried diets will drink more because they are not having the water

content of meat. If you change an adult dog on to soya protein diet, do so gradually over three weeks, adding a little more each day to the ration it had previously. In this way, the intestine becomes adjusted and acquires the bacteria necessary to deal with a different type of feeding. You will notice an increase in the bulk of excreta with this type of feeding, at first, but this settles as the system adjusts. Many nutritional experts feel that the dog needs a large proportion of roughage in its diet to keep its intestines in good working order. They maintain that although the excreta from the low residue diets are easier to clean up these foods are not so beneficial to the dog. The wild dog and some working dogs still eat the entire body of their kill including fur, bones, and flesh. In this way they take in a great deal of roughage which we find it hard to provide in domestic conditions.

The addition of between a teaspoonful and two tablespoonsful (depending upon the size of the dog) of desiccated suet seems to aid the utilization of the food and leave less residual matter. As with humans, one dog will grow fat on what will leave another lean. It is sometimes quite difficult to account for all the food a dog has. It is a great pity to make a dog fat, to spoil its beauty and shorten its life. There are slimming diets for dogs which your vet will prescribe, but it is much wiser not to allow your pet to become overweight in the first place. Dogs do not need sugar and sweet things and should never acquire the taste for them. A small piece of cheese is a more suitable and much appreciated titbit. Some types of soft, moist meat retailed in block form are preserved in sugar and are an undesirable food for a dog with a tendency to obesity or diabetes. You should always try to find out the ingredients of any new dog food, with the same concern that you would nor-

41

mally expect to show for your own food.

There is no harm at all in giving the dog the occasional potato left from family meals as part of the carbohydrate content of its diet. Some dogs will enjoy carrots and green vegetables, but there is no need to prepare them specially for it. Dogs do not need fruit, because they synthesize vitamin C within their own bodies, but some will pick raspberries and blackberries, and most enjoy apples. At times most dogs will have a compulsion to eat grass as an emetic, and will take the leaves from house plants if no grass is available. In spring they will graze on lush new grass and digest it, but during the rest of the year they use it only to make themselves vomit.

Large, unsplintered marrowbones are a treat, and also exercise the dog's teeth and its jaw muscles. My dogs disregard bones while they are fresh, seeming to prefer them 'hung' for a few days before they merit attention. A bone is a very precious thing to a dog and even dogs that are very good friends should be given their bones in separate rooms. Neither bones nor water and feed bowls should be left in the garden over night, because they may be contaminated by rat urine. Fish, rabbit, and poultry bones are well known to be dangerous because they splinter, but my dogs have on occasion opened the refrigerator and consumed a whole chicken without ill-effect except to the family who expected to have it for dinner. It may be that the bones of young broiler chicken are dissolved by the gastric juices, so do not panic if the dog eats one by accident, but do not feed them deliberately.

A dog should have one bowl for water and another for food; they should be the dog's only and washed up separately from the family plates. You should allow your dog no more than twenty minutes to eat its food before taking away what is left. You can easily teach it to bring its own bowl or to shake paws before meals to add to the importance of the occasion. Never tease by giving and taking away, once your dog has learned that it must always allow its owner to take anything from it without protest. One return of the yielded prize is enough; more is unkind and would provoke justifiable bad temper. Short-faced dogs cannot help making a little mess while eating and it is a good idea to place a sheet of newspaper on the floor. Dogs will not eat outside if they are distracted by passing people, if they are wet and cold, nor will a male eat if he senses a bitch in season. Stud dogs in a kennel often lose condition while bitches are in oestrus because food is of secondary interest at that time. In some breeds it is customary to place the feeding dish on a box or a stool so that the dog can stand erect to eat. This encourages a good front and shoulders. Dogs with fringed ears may have them protected by an old stocking while they are eating; Old English sheepdogs and Saint Bernards wear bibs to protect the coat from drips. However the meal is taken it should be happily anticipated and joyously presented. Afterwards most owners find it useful to continue the puppy-training habit of sending the dog straight into the garden when it has finished.

GROOMING

Many people enjoy grooming dogs. If you do not enjoy this type of work, however, or have not the time to give to it, then you should choose a smooth-coated breed which demands minimal care. Unfortunately, dogs are often chosen from show specimens or from book illustrations which show dogs that have hours daily spent on their coats. The pet dog in normal family circumstances is seldom going to look so glamorous, and it is better to trim down a long coat to manageable length than to keep it full and bedraggled. Poodles are very expensive to keep, because they need regular, professional clipping, unless you are prepared to take lessons yourself, in which case you will also need some convenient place in which to do a rather mess-making job. The harsh-coated terrier breeds, the wire-haired fox terrier, and the Airedale, for example, require to be stripped of their dead coat periodically. For show purposes this is done in the traditional way, that is, plucked out by finger and thumb. It is a slow, tiring business, bound to be expensive on professional time, and the pet terrier is likely to be machine clipped at more reasonable cost. Very long-coated breeds, such as the Afghan, the Maltese terrier, and the Yorkshire terrier will almost certainly have to have coat length restricted. The show 'Yorkie' spends a good deal of its life done up in oil and curling papers, and could not be allowed to indulge its natural sporting instincts for fear of spoiling its ground-length coat.

The average pet dog needs grooming to keep its hair and skin clean, and to remove dead hair so that it does not make too much mess in the house. The Old English sheepdog, which has become so popular as a pet would not live indoors at all in its correct situation, and it may suffer skin irritation through being too warm. Congealed food around the face, faeces dried under the tail, knots of hair in the undercoat can make a beautiful creature quite repulsive. Remember, then, that the dog you have seen in the picture or at the show did not get like that without a great deal of work, and it was probably being brushed until the moment before the camera flashed or the dog was put in the ring.

Today, we are keeping as pets many dogs that formerly lived out-of-doors in cold conditions bedded in straw or woodwool that does a lot to clean the coat. In natural conditions the dog would shed its coat twice a year, the temperature and duration of daylight affecting the life of the hair. If we keep dogs in centrally heated houses, lit for as much as eighteen hours a day, we must expect coat to be shed throughout the year, and daily grooming is necessary to keep the dog socially acceptable. The owner of the dog who grumbles that the dog leaves hairs all over the furniture is admitting that the way in which the dog has been groomed and trained is at fault. There are still times of the year when the dog will shed hair in quantity, and the bitch often loses coat after a real or imaginary pregnancy. The best thing to do is to take the dog into the garden and remove the dead coat in one go. It is useless to try to 'save' it, and it is less messmaking to have one stripping session than a little hair out every day, and the new coat will grow in faster once the old is away. Labradors, corgis, and Dalmatians shed some coat throughout the year.

Puppies should be taught from earliest days that they have to be groomed. The toy dogs should stand or lie on a table, and the bigger dogs must stand still on the floor. Any pet dog must be capable of allowing its owner to examine it in any possible way. You must be able to clean the ears, open the mouth, pick up the feet, and comb and brush the dog all over. If your dog does not allow you to do any of these things, then the dog is master, and you are not. If you find that your pet suddenly resents a particular area being touched, then you should suspect some special sensitivity or injury to the part, and investigate further. If a previously docile dog will not allow grooming, or exhibits any marked personality change, it is important to consult your veterinary surgeon, because dogs, like people, become irritable when incubating infections or suffering pain. Unless you know the dog has had some recent experience to make it wary of handling, you owe it to the dog to have bad temper investigated.

Grooming equipment varies from breed to breed. When you buy your puppy from a specialist you will be told the type of brush and the size number of the comb that suits the type of hair best. Smooth-coated breeds require a brush, ranging from baby-soft for the chihuahua, to quite stiff for the large dogs. A final polish can be given with a piece of real silk or velvet. Dead hair is removed from smooth coats with a hound glove, that is, a mitt with a palm section of short wire or fibre bristles, but an ordinary household rubber glove will remove a surprising amount of loose hair. With some dogs loose hair and dust can be removed with a vacuum cleaner.

The silky coated, small breeds should be taught from puppy days to lie on their sides, on a table or the owner's lap, so that tangles in the coat may be combed out carefully. Very good quality, smooth-toothed combs should be used, and many breeders invest in a fine quality 'human' hairbrush to avoid breaking the coat. Small tangles taken out daily prevent having to cut away a matted mass. Hair under the tail and on the sheath of the male may be lightly trimmed to avoid unpleasant smells. White breeds such as the Maltese terrier, and Cavaliers with a high proportion of white markings look beautiful after a bath, which may be given every six to eight weeks in these breeds, provided the natural oil is not dried out of the coat. Surplus hair should be trimmed out from between the pads of the feet, and many pet dogs in the long-coated breeds will have the tops of the feet trimmed too. It renders the dog unfit for the show ring but saves a lot of mud brought into the house.

Labrador retrievers, collies, and Pomeranians are among the breeds with a dense, waterproof undercoat which should not be combed, except when it is being shed. A good brushing of the top coat is all that is needed for daily grooming. Terriers thrive on brushing with a stiff, coarse brush.

Smooth-coated breeds need very little bathing, and once or twice a year is enough unless the dog has rolled in something unpleasant. You should always use a shampoo made for dogs, and not one intended for human hair which has a different formula. Never for any reason use a detergent. There are many good dog shampoos available, as well as some antiparasite treatments which are sponged on to the coat and left to dry without rinsing.

The smaller dog is best bathed in the kitchen sink, and dried with towels or a hair dryer if it does not object to the noise. Take care that it does not go into the garden and roll in mud immediately after – there seems to be a strong incentive to do this. The big dog is best tethered on the lawn in hot weather, surrounded by an assortment of bowls and cans of tepid water, with which it can be sponged down, rather than immersed. A walk on the lead will dry the dog off. Rainwater is good for the dog's coat and it does not hurt it to get wet provided it is dried quickly afterwards. Many dogs love to be played with under a sprinkler or garden hose in the summer. The short-coated, indoor dog may be cleaned with a damp chamois leather to remove surface dust, and facial wrinkles should be sponged clean.

Several aids to dry-cleaning may be bought, but powdered starch is the cheapest. Dry-cleaning with starch is messy because it must be well brushed out, but it is useful for young puppies which should not be bathed before they are four months old, and for the very old dog. Dry-cleaning is also useful to improve the appearance of the white markings of a red-and-white or brindle-and-white dog. These markings are often dressed with chalk for shows, but this should be washed off immediately after showing, because it tends to rot the coat. Houseproud owners will want to wash and dry the feet of long-coated dogs after walks. The dog may be taught as a puppy to be co-operative to the extent of waiting on the doormat and presenting each leg in turn. Never put disinfectant in the washing water; it is unnecessary and may cause severe degeneration of the nails and pads.

In snowy weather ice is apt to ball on the feet of long-coated dogs; be sure to inspect the feet and remove it. Of course, grooming is essential for a beautiful shining coat, but at least half of the dog's beauty comes from inside, with the good health that results from correct and balanced feeding. Coat texture is hereditary, and some strains within a breed may need more fat or more of one vitamin and so on to give the desired effect. The breeder from whom you bought the dog can give the best advice on the familial requirements.

It is wise to examine the mouth of the very old dog daily, to ensure that its gums are healthy, and that food particles are not being trapped in slack tissue. Teeth become covered in tartar and need periodical scaling by the veterinary surgeon. Dogs' teeth do decay, resulting in foul breath, and preventing them from enjoying their food. Older dogs of the heavy breeds may grow horny patches on the pressure points on front and back legs. Benzyl benzoate emulsion rubbed into these patches will soften them and the dog should be given extra bedding and not encouraged to lie on concrete paving out-of-doors. The ears of all breeds must be kept clean, otherwise accumulated wax provides an ideal breeding ground for parasites. Wax may be softened with a little warmed olive oil put in by a dropper, and the debris gently removed with cotton wool held in forceps. Never probe into the ear deeper than the region which you can see. Your veterinary surgeon can also supply you with medicated ear drops to use regularly. Any excess of hair growing within the ear should be gently removed with tweezers.

Some breeds have slightly protruding eyes which exude some moisture; the surrounding area should be kept clean with cotton wool. Profuse discharge from the eye indicates a disorder, either a conjunctivitis or a malformation of the eyelid or eyelashes which is causing irritation. Only your veterinary surgeon can advise you. Some breeds have a hereditary malformation of the eye shape, involving turning in, or turning out of the eyelid, known respectively as *entropion* and *ectropion*. The condition may be corrected surgically in the interest of comfort for the dog, but not for exhibition purposes, and such an animal should not be bred from. In breeds where the animal's facial structure changes radically during the first two years of life, as, for example, the boxer's does when the dog is acquiring its 'stop' or face shortening, the eyelid irritation may correct itself when the adult face is formed.

Dewclaws are situated just above the foot on the inside of the leg, and are removed from many breeds soon after birth. If dewclaws remain, inspect them regularly to make sure that they do not grow around and penetrate the leg. Feet should be examined regularly to ensure that there are no small cysts forming between the toes, a common ailment in the dog. Young puppies not taking much outdoor exercise should have their toenails cut, well below the quick. The breeder will have been doing this weekly since birth, so that the pup should not make much fuss about it, unless you cut too closely, when bleeding may be stopped quickly with a dab of friar's balsam (tincture of benzoin). Adult dogs' nails should stay short by exercise on roads, beaches, or gravel areas, but if they become very overgrown it is safest to ask a vet or a trimming parlour to clip them. The very elderly dog seems to experience an accelerated rate of nail growth which may inhibit walking.

When you are grooming your pet you have the opportunity to spot defects early, to feel for lumps and bumps. A quick look at the dog's anus will ensure that no inflammation of the anal glands has time to build up. Mature bitches should have the mammary glands examined regularly to see that no tumours are forming around the nipples or in the glands themselves. A nodule there needs veterinary investigation as soon as possible. Skin irritations of all kinds show up on the hairless area of the abdomen, a part frequently hidden unless you roll your dog over for inspection.

Fleas congregate on the back just in front of the tail, or in the warm folds between the back legs. Look for the oval brown flea, or the black dust of flea excreta. A very fine-toothed nit comb should be used on the coat near the tail, because if fleas are present you can usually surprise one there. The really effective way to kill the fleas you catch is to crack them between your thumb nails, or to place the contents of the comb in a dish of methylated spirits. It is important to rid your dog of fleas, not only for social reasons and the irritation it causes, but also because some dogs are allergic to the bite of a flea and will carry a skin condition long after the parasite is gone. The flea is also the host of the tapeworm egg, and if the dog catches its own fleas, it will probably become infested. The most effective flea powders are only obtainable through veterinary surgeons, and it is worth the extra expense and effort to get a really scientifically produced preparation, with which you may also treat the dog's bed, and any carpets on which it lies. The family cat should be treated too, but with a powder specially formulated for cats. Special anti-flea collars are sold but I am doubtful of the wisdom of using them, and think it indicates an owner not willing to take enough personal trouble with the pet.

Around the ears and ear flap lice may be found, particularly in the young puppy. It is important to get rid of these tiny parasites because they suck the blood of the host and may cause anaemia. A course of medicated baths, supplied by your veterinary surgeon, will effect a cure. Ticks thrive in summer, when they may be picked up from long grass. They will appear on the dog like a flat brown seed embedded in the skin, but as they fill up with blood they make quite a big lump. With great care the end of the tick may be touched with methylated spirit. The tick will release its hold and may be removed with tweezers. Any attempt to pull a tick out untreated in some way will result in the head being left in the skin. When you have removed the tick, remember to clean the dog's skin with antiseptic. The daily grooming, and your observation of the dog's behaviour will help you prevent an invasion of any of these parasites before they become widespread.

HOUSING

The pet dog will normally live in the house and you should decide upon the pattern the puppy's life will take before you buy it. The kitchen and utility room is the obvious place for the dog to spend the greater part of the day if someone is working there. There are usually tiled floors in these rooms which are easy to clean, and they usually permit easy access to the garden. Bitches in season must also be confined to an easily cleaned area because their bloodstained discharge will mark carpets and leave a lingering dog-discernible odour. A dog

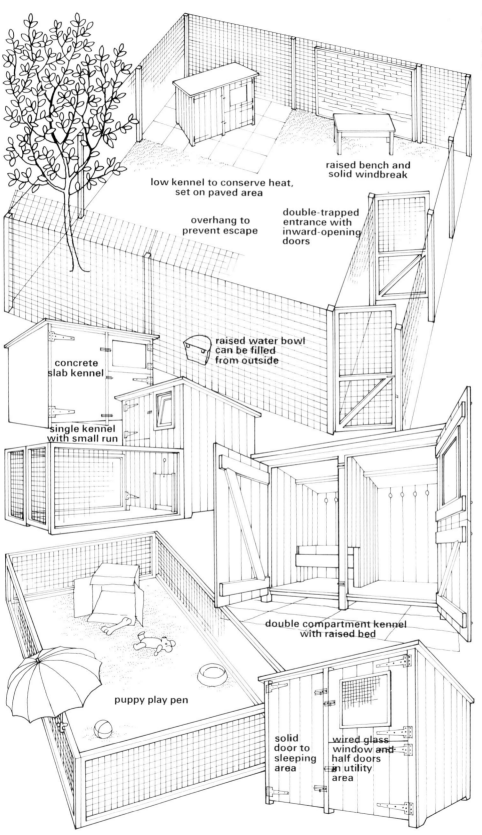

Well-designed kennels and runs are more comfortable for the dog and are easier for the owner to maintain.

raised bench and solid windbreak

low kennel to conserve heat, set on paved area

overhang to prevent escape

double-trapped entrance with inward-opening doors

raised water bowl can be filled from outside

concrete slab kennel

single kennel with small run

double compartment kennel with raised bed

puppy play pen

solid door to sleeping area

wired glass window and half doors in utility area

46

needs a bed that it can call its own; preferably one in both kitchen and living room, if you want to keep it off the furniture. It is not wise, hygienic or comfortable to allow a dog to sleep on your own bed after its early puppy days, but many people like to have a dog sleep in its own place in the bedroom, feeling the benefit of companionship and protection. Some adult dogs prefer a bed on the landing where they may keep an eye on all doors, but this is only permissible for the perfectly house-trained. It is not kind, nor does it make much sense as a burglar deterrent, to put a single dog out to sleep in a kennel. If you have two young dogs together it may be easier to have them in during the day and in a kennel to sleep, to save wear and tear on your kitchen quarters, but kennel dogs do not house-train so quickly and will be more excitable when they are brought into the house. Kennels should be solidly built, and well insulated. If heating is to be provided it must be very carefully installed so that there is no chance of a mischievous dog reaching electric wiring, or overturning stoves. For small dogs, the type of electric heater used in bathrooms may be positioned high on the wall and directed down towards them. Dogs hate draughts, and doors and windows must fit well. A deep box higher than the dog's back should be provided as the actual sleeping place on a floor area twice as large as the bed. Woodwool makes the best bedding for outside kennels and may be bought by the bale. Wood shavings or chippings are also available. Straw and hay are best avoided, because they may be infected by rats and harbour parasites.

The public health authorities in Britain are advising against the use of wooden kennels, which will gradually be phased out for breeder's use, leaving the choice of brick, steel, concrete, or asbestos kennelling. Should you decide that part of a garage might be made into dog housing, take care that the dogs are safely partitioned off from the many poisonous and allergy-producing substances normally kept in garages. The pool of sump oil on the floor or around a drain can be a long-term killer. Also, heavy vapours given off from boilers can suffocate a dog.

Dogs sleeping outside need not be completely shut in if they have a draught-protected door to a run with solid, windproof sides. This kind of arrangement makes cleaning easier in boarding kennels, and it eases the claustrophobic dogs, but is not to be recommended in an urban situation because it makes for more noise and barking. If you have two dogs and a garden too big to fence completely, then it is useful to have an enclosed, paved or concreted run for them where they may be safely put for short periods. Dogs can jump to great heights, and the fencing of the run needs to be very high, or roofed over, or at best have an 18-inch (45-centimetre) strip of wire netting fixed horizontally at the top of the fence, so that the dog cannot climb out. Dogs may become very adept at opening latches and gate catches. Strong bolts are the best answer for my boxers, because I have found that they can operate anything of the push-down, handle type. For big dogs the wire for the run must be heavy gauge. Unfortunately, chicken wire or light chain link unravel like knitting. Most dogs dig, and fencing must be embedded in concrete, or pegged down with steel wire pegs at frequent intervals to prevent them from escaping underneath. If you intend to leave the dogs in a run in summer, some shade by a tree or canopy must be provided, and they also like a low platform on which to lie. If the area is windy, some of the perimeter fencing should be solid to make a windbreak, and the entrance of the kennel should face away from the prevailing wind. When siting the kennel within the enclosure, think ahead to what the dogs will do. A kennel that slopes towards towards the back makes an easy place to jump on to lie in the sun, but put it too near the fence and it is another easy leap down the other side. We prefer low kennels, which are difficult to clean but do help conserve heat for the dogs. A dog should never be shut in a small kennel in hot weather, because even with open windows the temperature rises dramatically.

Water must always be provided in runs, in a removable vessel which can be scrubbed clean. Stale, tepid water is an invitation to disease, as is water contaminated by the saliva of short-faced breeds. A fire extinguisher in working order and readily available is a sensible accessory to a kennel. Excreta deposited in a kennel run must be picked up regularly, and a covered run should be hosed down with a weak disinfectant solution frequently. When using any disinfectants near dogs dilute the liquid strictly as directed, because pads may be burned and allergies caused by the indiscriminate use of caustic chemicals. If dogs are being wormed, extra attention should be paid to removing excreta and cleaning the area, or worm eggs will remain.

There are many commercially made dog beds that may be purchased for the pet kept in the house, they are all liable to be damaged in the early years, however. The traditional basket is liked by most dogs but it is easily destroyed and difficult to clean. I do not care for the beds of the canvas hammock type suspended from a folding iron frame. The frame becomes weak with use and may trap a paw with its scissor mechanism. The canvas also tends to sag under a heavy dog. Rigid polythene beds are scrubbable and useful for smaller dogs, and the very large breeds love a covered foam-rubber mattress on which they can stretch, but it may get torn up in puppy days. We find that for most breeds a hardwood box, home carpentered or made to order is the most satisfactory bed. Back and sides should be high enough to support the dog, and the timber should be thick enough to stand a little chewing on the corner posts. A support underneath should raise the bed from the floor; such a bed may be specially made to fit a useful space, next to the central-heating boiler being the favourite. Wooden beds which may be scrubbed clean with bleach and then rinsed in clean water, and dried in the sun are undoubtedly the most hygienic. Indoor bedding needs only to be something soft to lie on, something washable or easily disposable. Carpet pieces make good box lining provided the dog is not allergic to man-made fibre or to the dye used. Old eiderdowns and pillows are particularly luxurious but if they are torn up the feathers are very messy indeed. Rooms where the dog can be supervised may have more decorative beds with travelling rugs or blankets. It is not wise to allow your pet freedom of the house until you are sure you can rely on its behaviour; you cannot blame a puppy for damage if it is allowed the opportunity to get at precious things. The kitchen area is the easiest to render dog-proof, with everything put out of reach. Low cupboards need to have dog-proof catches, particularly those which contain bleaches, detergents, polishes, and so on. Cakes of soap also present a danger,

especially to the wide-mouthed, short-faced breeds. Soap is attractive to dogs because of its fat content. Many dogs will lap soapy water and will snatch a cake of soap and choke on it if it is small enough to get wedged in the back of the throat.

Your dog should not wear a collar when shut up alone in the kitchen; the collar may become caught on a handle with tragic results. Collars and leads should not be worn in the car for the same reasons. The new puppy will teach all the family to be tidy, because anything left within its reach will be taken. Children's plastic toys are a danger to puppies; they may swallow pieces which will obstruct the stomach or bowel but may not show on an X-ray. Nylon stockings and tights are another danger, as are plastic bags. The favourite dog toy is a ball, but be sure that it is big enough not to be swallowed in the excitement of play. Toys containing squeakers excite some dogs to the point of hysteria; such toys are always dismembered in the end, and you must take care that the squeak is not swallowed. Most dogs enjoy the strips of hide which are sold in varying shapes for them to chew on. If large pieces are eaten they are usually vomited back quite quickly. Dogs left alone will chew things, and many a dog has cut off the family's telephone. Great care should be taken that electric wiring apparatus is well out of the way, and that gas cooker taps cannot be turned on. The lever type of refrigerator and door handle is easily operated by the tall dog, and many homes have had to change to the old-fashioned type of round handle.

Some people are able to maintain a beautiful garden and a dog, either by making a wire edging to the flower beds, or by persistently training the dog to keep off the borders, and curbing mole-digging on the lawn. If you have two large dogs, the garden never looks quite the same again. They are bound to have chasing games and play stalking among the shrubs. It is a matter of deciding priorities and it is a pity if there is constant recrimination against the dogs. Small dogs are much less violent in play. It is antisocial not to have your garden fenced well enough to keep your dog inside it, but do discourage well-meaning neighbours who may offer titbits and attract a dog to the fence. Your dog barking at neighbours when they come out into their

Choose the collar in keeping with your dog's character, and have several leads to suit different activities. Beds may be practical or luxurious. Coats for the elderly or invalid dog are cut so that they protect the chest.

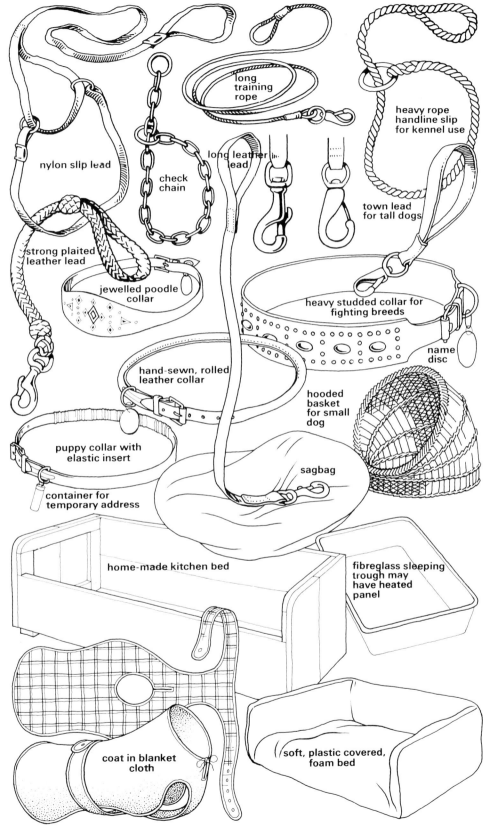

long training rope

heavy rope handline slip for kennel use

nylon slip lead

check chain

long leather lead

town lead for tall dogs

strong plaited leather lead

jewelled poodle collar

heavy studded collar for fighting breeds

name disc

hand-sewn, rolled leather collar

hooded basket for small dog

puppy collar with elastic insert

sagbag

container for temporary address

home-made kitchen bed

fibreglass sleeping trough may have heated panel

coat in blanket cloth

soft, plastic covered, foam bed

Left The Skye terrier was bred to hunt martens, otters, and badgers.

Below 'Westie' puppies must have their coats correctly groomed from an early age.

Above **Eager, bright, intelligent, little border terriers.**

Right Smooth fox terrier.

gardens does not win you any friends, and does not need to happen if you have trained it properly. Dogs must be kept off all roads, however quiet, and it is wise to fit self-closing catches to gates. If a large dog is free behind a solid, closed gate it is only reasonable to have a notice warning persons outside, who may even be afraid of friendly dogs. The most amiable of animals is likely to behave in uncharacteristic manner if someone shows fear of it. If you wish to make a habit of taking your dog with you to answer a knock at the door, it is a good idea to have a waist-high gate to the porch, such as a stable type door, so that an eager dog does not slip out. The nervous caller can talk to you over the fence and has no need to come in contact with the dog which has been trained to do sentry duty in the doorway until told that the caller may enter. This kind of work needs little teaching to the guarding breeds.

By law your dog must wear a collar and a name tag engraved with the owner's name and address (and telephone number if possible) when outside the home. For the dog on holiday, a little tube can be bought to attach to the collar and the holiday address may be slipped inside. It is also possible to have a dog permanently tattooed with an identification number which is kept by a registration organization. The tattoo is painless, and is done on the inside of the thigh, and does not disfigure the dog.

Collars are very much breed symbols – terriers and bull breeds wear studded ones, poodles diamond-encrusted models. First collars are soon outgrown, and should be very light, inexpensive ones; the cat collar which has an inset of elastic is very suitable. Breeds for which an arched neck is a feature of their beauty should wear narrow, sewn collars, or chains which rest low on the neck. An unnecessarily wide, heavy collar can make an elegant dog look ungainly. The check chain collar which pulls up tight when the lead is attached is excellent for thick necked breeds if it is properly fitted and used. For exercise in country areas the older, obedient dog may only need a light nylon show lead which incorporates a collar and is quickly put on and released. These coloured leads are washable and hard wearing, but they are not suitable in built-up areas because they may be slipped off. If you enter your dog into a show, even one at

a summer fête, it looks professional to have a lead of this type which indicates that you have good control of the dog, and also hides nothing of its conformation. Leads must be appropriate to breed and have good strong hooks; we favour the older type of hook, not the automatic types which become unsafe when they weaken. Harnesses are strictly disapproved of nowadays, even for the tiniest dogs. They allow the dog to pull, because you cannot apply restrictive pressure to the ribs as you can to the neck, and a dog constantly leaning into a harness distorts its shoulders and places a strain on the heart.

Coats should only be used for very young, sick, and very old dogs. If a coat is needed, it should completely cover the body including the chest. The type which only covers the back does little good, and may even do harm. The only time a healthy dog requires a coat is if it has to stand about for a long time after leaving a hot atmosphere, for example, after rail travel or dogs going home from a show. Except for preserving the coat on the way to a show, dogs need no wet weather protection at all; mackintoshes and bootees make the animal look and feel ridiculous.

Owning a dog means you have to take special care for its safety – like a young child a dog is unaware of most dangers. A puppy will try to eat practically everything, certainly its first few weeks will be occupied in exploratory chews around the garden. Some very ordinary plants can be toxic to the dog, causing disturbance to the central nervous system, exhibited by mouth-foaming, coma, or collapse. Bulbs of all the spring flowers are poisonous, and the dog should not be allowed to dig them up or even be close by when you are planting. The leaves of foxglove and peony, tomato and potato, and many commonly cultivated shrubs such as azalea, wisteria, and privet are also toxic. House plants are often chewed, for mischief or as a substitute for grass. Philodendron, mother-in-law's tongue, and poinsettia are among the most dangerous, and may cause swelling of the mouth tissues and asphyxiation.

Dangerous substances often left unattended in non-dog owning households include moth balls and bleaches – dogs even drink out of WC pans, so beware if you are using a strong cleaner. No effective rat poison can be considered safe for dogs, and even those commonly provided for household use have a cumulative effect. A dog seen to eat poisoned bait should have veterinary treatment at once. Dogs should not play with dead rats, or with birds that may have taken poisoned seed, nor should they eat fallen apples that may have been fouled by rats, because rat urine carries deadly disease. Dogs are greatly attracted to hedgehogs, and will roll them about. The hedgehog carries fleas and is best gently removed from the vicinity. The dog should be treated for parasites at once. The stinging nettle can bring a smooth-coated puppy up in weals, as it does on human skin. Horse and cow manure is very attractive to dogs, and beyond causing a temporary looseness of the bowels, does not seem to do harm, but constant access to manure you have stacked will be a nuisance. Lead poisoning is a danger, and you should check the content of paint which is used on doors likely to be chewed. Slug bait is fatal if eaten and must never be used in a dog owner's garden. Weed-killing sprays of all kinds cause from mild to very serious stomach upsets. The dog can obtain a considerable quantity of any substance through licking its paws, and does not have to actually eat poison to be affected. Farm sprays are considerably stronger than those sold to the public, and the wind may carry spray over a considerable area. Look well ahead when you are on country walks. The vapour from newly creosoted wood is persistent, and you should never put dogs into a newly treated kennel. Carbolic disinfectants must be carefully used at recommended strengths. You should take great precautions with any aerosol presented preparations, because the fine vapour can get into the dog's eyes and nose, causing acute pain, and even damage to sight.

Never have a dog free with you when you are mowing the lawn. It may get in the way, and cause an accident to one or both of you. Stones thrown up by the blades of a rotary mower may travel quite a distance at dog level and your pet is better off indoors.

It is possible to become over-concerned about the safety of the dog, and to restrict it so much would be no pleasure to the dog or its owner, but it is as well to be aware of the substances that present hazards, especially while the pup is young. A swimming pool in the garden is a definite danger until the dog is aware of it, particularly a pool which is lightly covered in winter. Special care should be taken if there is a fall of snow when boundary marks will be obliterated. Dogs will rush on to ice with great delight, but if they go through they may not find their way out again if help is not to hand, and even strong swimmers have drowned this way. When you own a pup you must train yourself to think ahead to what might happen, and then act quickly before it does.

You will learn to be tidy, to keep doors closed, and to live above dog level. If you are not prepared to make this much adjustment, you will not have your dog for long. While thinking of care for your dog, the single owner, or the small family must face the fact that some disaster could leave the dog without owners, particularly in the event of a car accident. Prudent owners will leave a note of their wishes in their wills, naming someone to decide about the dog, in the light of its age and circumstances at the time. Only someone who knows the dog well is able to judge whether it will be able to become adjusted to another home or whether it would be kinder to have the dog destroyed. In the case of large dogs, or several dogs, do realize that pending a decision these dogs will cost money, and a small sum should be made available for their keep if you hope they may be found other homes.

DOG FIGHTS

Dogs are animals with very strong instincts for possession, and they will fight on occasion. Some males are always looking for trouble, and their freedom must be restricted because they cannot be allowed to interfere with more peaceable dogs and their owners. The last resort is the wearing of a muzzle, or the vet may be consulted about having the dog castrated. The discerning owner will be able to differentiate between the noise and rough play type of fight which inflicts little injury, serving only to establish pecking order, and the real fight with intent to kill. The first type of fight is best ignored and resolved by the dogs themselves, especially if they are to meet often, otherwise the contest lingers on.

Dealing with the savage fight is a much discussed question. If a distraction can be provided, such as ringing the door bell,

Above An Irish setter in all the glory of its distinctive colouring. *Left* The Weimaraner, once exclusively bred by German aristocracy, is now growing in favour as a guard dog and for police work. *Right* The English springer spaniel is a good all-purpose gundog that requires plenty of exercise if kept as a pet.

throwing a brick at a metal surface, even the voices of strangers, a brief lull may enable one dog to be removed from the scene. A bucket of water helps for small dogs, or the garden hose directed as a jet for bigger ones. If the dogs are wearing collars, as habitual fighters must, you may be able to twist one and temporarily cut off the dog's air supply, so that the dog must open its mouth and let go. Pulling ears, gripping testicles (not too roughly) have all proved useful, but you must follow up with quick action and get the dogs apart and under control, otherwise they will begin again. Effort should be made to force the dogs to let go rather than have one owner pull a dog away while the other dog has a grip, or dreadful injuries may result.

Stopping a fight is largely a matter of improvisation at the time; shrieking does not help, nor does laying about you with a stick, because a fighting dog is oblivious to that amount of pain. Snatching a small dog up in your arms is most unwise because you expose its vulnerable hairless underbelly to the enemy and may get yourself bitten too. If you are bitten or scratched at all it is wise to check on your antitetanus injection programme because any animal bite may become infected. After a fight the dog should be rested, bleeding staunched, and the actual damage assessed. Some wounds will need stitching, but the small, punctured tooth wound is more dangerous in that greater damage has been done to the underlying tissue.

CARE OF THE BITCH

If you have chosen a bitch puppy, you should be expecting her first season when she is about eight months old, with individual and breed variations. Veterinary advice should be sought if the bitch has not had her first season by the time she is eighteen months old, because her metabolism may be out of balance in some way. The on-coming season is heralded by an increased excitement and awareness, even irritability which you will come to recognize. After this comes the swelling of the vulva, the outer genital area, and then the onset of the bloodstained discharge.

The time when the bitch is most vulnerable for mating is from ten to fifteen days after the start of the red discharge, usually when it is turning to a colourless fluid. A male dog becomes aware and begins paying attention quite early unless he is a professional stud dog that seldom takes an interest until the correct day for mating. Bitches in season should be kept off carpets and furniture, and do not need to be taken out for exercise. They certainly should not be taken into other people's homes, or public places. If they must go out, they are best carried to a car to avoid leaving a trail. The restriction that a bitch's season makes in her home routine is one of the best arguments for spaying, that is, having your veterinary surgeon remove part or all of her reproductive organs as soon as it is suitable, after her first season. It is possible to have a bitch spayed earlier, but the bitch may remain immature both physically and mentally. Performing a hysterectomy on the bitch is still a major operation, but with improved anaesthetic equipment and provision for small animal surgery now so widespread, it is considered to be a very good risk operation, and the bitch should be fully recovered within a few days.

Drugs are available which will delay a bitch's heat period, but veterinary opinion is very divided on the wisdom of their use, because interfering with hormone balance is not always beneficial. Your veterinary surgeon will advise you on oestrus control, and can also bring about an abortion if a mismating should have occurred, provided the bitch is taken to the vet within twenty-four hours of the mismating. It has been thought better not to abort a bitch more than once if you wish to breed again. It is better to let her have the crossbred litter, saving only one or two of the pups to take care of the mental and physical needs of the bitch.

A pedigree bitch which has had one crossbred litter may, of course, be put to stud of her own kind later. It is not true that one crossbred litter will linger on and affect a bitch for life. Bitches kept together seem to trigger off seasons in one another, and they will take turns in attempting to mount each other. Such behaviour is natural and should be ignored unless they become irritated, in which case they should be separated or have tranquillizers prescribed so that their instincts become less intense.

It is difficult for the ordinary family home to be able to accommodate an in-season bitch and a male dog. Both can get into quite uncharacteristic feverish states at the height of sexual excitement, and it requires constant vigilance and strong iron bars to keep big breed dogs apart. Any dog will mate any bitch that is ready, and perform strange physical contortions to do so. Do not trust to divergence in size, or close family relationship as a method of canine birth control. A dog will mate his mother, his sister, or any other relation, and he will mate a bitch that completely dominates him in any other situation, indeed, she will actively encourage him to do so. Generally, if you are to have a dog and bitch in the household, one must be sexually neutered, or one must be boarded out for the three to four weeks of the bitch's heat period.

A very maternally minded bitch that has not been mated may show all signs of pregnancy, including enlargement of the mammary glands, secretion of milk, and mock labour pains. In fact, this false pregnancy is so like a real one that even experienced breeders are deceived until the last minute. The condition in the unmated bitch is termed a *phantom pregnancy*. It is likely that she will take a toy into her bed to cuddle, be extremely distressed and off her food. She may even be irritable and fiercely protective to the litter that only she can see. Hormone treatments are sometimes prescribed to relieve the bitch but with my own I try to provide more exercise, diversions, cut food a little, and let them work their way out of it. If you are thinking of getting another puppy or a kitten, when the bitch is in phantom pregnancy is the ideal time. Having a litter does not cure distressing phantoms, only an ovario-hysterectomy will do that.

BOARDING KENNELS

It is always wise to establish a good relationship with a boarding kennel, because even if you mean to take your dog on holiday with you, there may be times when you will need to put it into care, especially in an emergency. It is very hard for a middle-aged dog to understand being kennelled for the first time and it must feel absolutely abandoned. The first choice for boarding is the kennel at which your dog was bred. They have the most interest in it, and probably own its relatives. Failing this, the breeder

may be able to send you to a kennel known to understand and have sympathy with your breed of dog. Not all dog people like or can deal with all dogs; the breeds vary so much in their requirements, their attitude to life, and their temperaments that it makes sense to go to a kennel where your kind of dog is understood, and where the security arrangements are suitable for the capabilities of your dog. In Britain, boarding kennels are licensed and inspected by local authorities, to ensure that they comply with the statutory requirements for the comfort of the animal, and particularly with regard to fire precautions.

Boarding kennels appreciate the owner who asks to be allowed to make an inspection when they are comparatively empty early in the season, not when the kennels are full of animals that must not be excited. The best kennels fill up early for peak periods, and you should book as soon as you know your own arrangements. Expect to pay a deposit on your booking, and to treat the kennel as you would your own hotel, warning early if you cannot take up the booking. Expect to take and collect your dog inside normal working hours, because boarding kennels seldom have night porters. It is best to arrange for the dog to arrive early in the day, so that it has time to assess the new surroundings and fellow boarders before being confined for the night. Most kennels will insist on seeing an inoculation certificate, with up to date booster doses. They will call a veterinary surgeon, for which you should expect to pay extra, for even a slight illness, because unqualified personnel are not permitted to prescribe for or treat an animal that is not their own property. Health vigilance is, of course, very much to your own advantage. Epidemics may spread very quickly in kennels.

Even the best of boarding kennels cannot console a dog that is devoted to its owner and desolated at being left. Such a dog may refuse to eat to the point of starvation, or its misery may trigger off a latent disease, especially in the middle-aged to elderly dog. The very old dog that is completely committed to its own household routine may be better off in the care of a 'sitter-in' or neighbour. In any case, a trial weekend in kennels well ahead of your holiday is a good idea and accustoms the dog to the pattern of being left and collected again. The younger dog

The Dobermann pinscher combines strength, power, and intelligence.

The Siberian husky is not an easy dog to keep as a pet.

Above The rough collie has been a favourite working dog and pet for many years.
Right The bearded collie is keen, affectionate, and tireless.

59

may thoroughly enjoy its time in kennels as an opportunity to fraternize with its own kind. Many dogs are completely tired out and will sleep for days on their return from kennels, showing they have had much more mental and physical activity than usual. Kennels vary in type from ones of army camp precision to more patched up, toy-strewn ones taking a few dogs on a friendly basis. Once the basics of watertight kennels, strong fencing, and good food are fulfilled the atmosphere depends entirely on the proprietors and their attitude to dogs in their care.

EXERCISE

Most people think that the word dog is almost synonymous with the word exercise. Indeed, one of the reasons for getting a dog is that the person feels that he or she is not getting enough walking, and feels out of place walking alone. The dog is not such a tyrant for formalized exercise as many people imagine; walking the dog should not be, need not be, a burden. Dogs imported into this country spend six months in quarantine where they never have more than a run in an exercise paddock, and they come out in good condition, sometimes taking show awards straight away. This is not to say that the converse is true, and that a dog need never go out, just that there is no need for a feeling of guilt if you don't want to turn out on a wet, cold day, or to deny yourself a dog because you cannot take it for long walks every day.

Unfortunately, people are always very anxious to exercise their new puppies, but this is the one time they really must not have any formalized exercise at all, because it is so easy to overstrain young bones and muscles. It is pitiful to see a young pup being dragged around the streets by children when it would be so much better off at free play in a garden. Small dogs can be very busy creatures and cover great distances around their own house and garden, or playing ball in the hall. Twenty minutes in the garden playing in an organized fashion with its owner is worth far more to the dog than being taken on the lead to a shopping centre. It is even worse to take your dog to the pub, particularly now that it has been found that passive smoking, inhaling the cigarette smoke of others does as much damage to the lungs of dogs as to humans'. Two dogs together give each other plenty of exercise, not only of limbs but jaw and neck muscles in tugging things between them and carrying great boughs of wood. Exercise should be fun, not plodding round the roads, raising a leg at every tree. Some breeds, the German shepherd dog, for instance, like to be taken at a brisk pace, or even a loping run, and dogs being brought into condition for show may even be exercised in a safe place while the owner rides a bicycle. Such hard exercise is not necessary for the average pet dog. Short-faced breeds are not equipped for long, sustained efforts and are best suited by being driven to an open space where they may run wild for a short time.

Most dogs love to swim and it is fine exercise for fronts and necks. The bigger hound breeds love to follow a horse. The scenting breeds will play hunt the slipper very cleverly, and the retriever will retrieve for you as long as you like to throw. In playing games suited to your dog's type, you are reinforcing its natural attributes and developing its latent talents. Even if your retriever never sees any game, it can be useful if you drop your car keys. The dog will find them for you if you have taught elementary scent discrimination, and you can do that on the living room floor on wet winter nights.

Dogs being shown, stud dogs, and pregnant bitches benefit from regular, steady walks, but in the main, exercise must be a pleasure, and not a duty, or neither dog nor owner will benefit. Almost every town has a dog training club which meets once a week. Both you and your dog will enjoy the social contact, whether you mean to progress to competition work or just afford your dog an opportunity to learn to behave in the face of maximum temptation. If you exercise your dog on unlit roads after dark, remember that it is almost invisible by your side, provide a luminous strip on its collar, and keep it on a short lead on the inside. Never let any dog, even an obedience champion, walk on a road or even a quiet lane off the lead. The canine mind can always be distracted at some point by an elemental temptation. The owners who boast that their pet does not need a lead are boosting their own ego at the risk of a dead dog on their conscience.

Training

When you buy your six-week-old puppy, it will have already been started in its education. The dam will have taught the pup to go away from the nest to defecate, she will have begun instruction in its bearing to other dogs and self-defence, and she will, by her own attitude have begun conditioning it to live with human beings. The breeder will probably have provided newspaper in the puppy run as a defecation area, so that it will be convenient for you to continue to put down newspaper in the kitchen for the times when it will be impossible for the pup to contain itself. Little puppies, like babies, cannot control themselves for long, and certainly not all night. It would be unfair to expect immaculate house behaviour before four months, perhaps longer in bad weather and if you have long nights. Those that rise early complete the house-training sooner; the puppy will certainly urinate on awakening, and if there are early morning noises where you live, it is best that you rise with them to let the puppy out. Puppies do not make use of an earth tray, as a kitten does, but remember that if you do adopt the pad of newspaper method a puppy cannot distinguish between today's unread edition and last weeks' intended for its use, and you must not leave wanted papers on the floor. Success or failure in house-training depends on the concentration you can give to the task. All dogs, except those with some defect of control or intellect, house-train eventually, but you will want it to be as quickly as possible. Mistakes in the early weeks, while you are around the house, are your fault and not the puppy's.

Puppies void on waking from sleep, immediately after taking food or drink, and probably also during play. It is up to you to watch for the hesitation, the questioning look, which means the urge has come. You will soon begin to recognize the actions. Then you take the puppy to the spot in the garden you have chosen as most useful, and say the signal word. We say 'Go and be good,' others say 'Hurry up,' but remember that too explicit a command can be em-barrassing in public. Taking into the garden may well distract the pup from the task it had in mind, and the only sensible way is to stay with it, urging it on, until it does defecate. Then you praise and hug your pet. Never push a young puppy out of the door alone, because you do not want to get cold and wet, and hope that the dog will know what it has gone out for. It will just sit against the door shivering, thinking you have turned suddenly very unkind, and will then relieve itself on coming back inside. Puppies' motions always seem to occur at inconvenient times, when you are holding a telephone conversation, cooking, or sitting to a meal, but their calls must be answered properly and promptly, for they cannot wait. Every mistake indoors delays house-training. Puppies are easier to house-train in summer, when doors are left open, but they may slow down when the colder weather comes and they find they must indicate that they want to go out. Most pups will walk to the door and stare at it, or pace about restlessly, but very few bark to ask, as their owners would like them to. As the puppy grows and achieves some measure of control you can avoid inconvenience by taking it outside, every one to one-and-a-half hours. The adult dog will probably manage on four garden visits a day. It is very useful indeed to have a dog that will perform to your word, especially if you mean to make the dog your constant companion, to travel and visit with you.

Mistakes indoors should be washed up quickly, to prevent the dog using the same spot again. When you have reason to think the dog could have indicated that it wanted to go out, then you are right to indicate your displeasure, the only way being by reprimand in a growling voice. For really flagrant rule-breaking, such as performing indoors after every opportunity given outside, then a sharp slap can be administered, only if caught in the act. If you come upon excrement or urine long after it was made, then it is useless to express more than distaste. If you have been out for some time and return

Above **Long-coated chihuahuas** are regarded as a separate breed from the smooth-coated by the Kennel Club – these toy dogs can be kept in situations which would be impossible for other breeds.

Left The **Cavalier King Charles spaniels** were once exclusively owned by the Duke of Marlborough – these gay, gregarious, small spaniels are adaptable to town or country life.

Right **Pugs** are dogs to be kept as individuals, making good household companions because of their intelligence.

to find the kitchen soiled, then it is definitely cruel to even mention it to a sensitive dog. What else could the dog do? Human beings cannot wait indefinitely either. An older dog suddenly losing control of urination needs veterinary attention and, of course, a dog suffering from any illness involving loose-ness of the bowels just cannot wait. Such mistakes should not be commented on, because the well-trained dog feels as much shame as a human at breaking house-training.

It is important to train your puppy to its name as soon as possible. If the family cannot agree on a name at first, call it 'Puppy', and this will stand as an alternative all its life – sometimes, in emergency, the only thing to jerk its memory. If you have chosen your pup early, the breeder will use for it the name you wish. I don't know whether it helps, but I always pick my puppies up, look them straight in the eyes, and say their name. Then use the name at every opportunity, prefacing any command with the animal's name. 'No!' is the most important word of all. It should be used from the first day you have the puppy in your home, and it will be 'No!' all the time at first. Persistent biting at forbidden things, after you have tried the distraction prin-ciple, will bring a 'No!' accompanied by a sharp but not violent slap. You will observe that the puppy's dam, or any other older dog will tolerate bad behaviour for just so long, and then reinforce her growl with a well-aimed paw but it is always on the instant of the act, and never prolonged. One sharp slap is a deterrent, indicating that doing that action brings something that hurts and makes her cross. Prolonged beating and loss of temper degrades only the human who inflicts it.

I find shouting rather difficult, and I very seldom raise my voice to my dogs, but when I am driven by exasperation to shout at them, the whole pack acts as if their world had come to an end. They will slink away, herd together, and show every sign of mortal fear. This attitude will last for an hour or more until we have 'made it up'. It pays to save extreme anger for very extreme misdeeds. The dog that is constantly shouted at may think that it is a normal human's tone and take very little notice.

The next most important thing to teach is for your puppy to come to your call,

Lead training and gaining control of your dog. The dog would rather play.

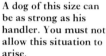

A dog of this size can be as strong as his handler. You must not allow this situation to arise.

64

instantly and always. This cast-iron obedience may save the dog's life, and possibly yours. For the solitary dog, training to come when called is best supplemented by making it worthwhile. Call it to its food, to be taken out, or to be cuddled. Titbits may be used as a form of bribery, but it may mean you always have to rattle the biscuit tin to get the dog indoors. As you would with a child, use some strategy. Call it when it was going to come anyway; persuade the puppy to feel that coming to you will always be pleasurable, for which it is worth leaving any other activity. Some dogs are enchanted by outdoors and are reluctant to come in while the sun shines. In this case, your best ploy is to go out yourself and both come in together.

The dog soon learns to tease, will come within arm's length and then dodge off again. If it is safe to do, the best action is to turn round and walk away. It will quickly deflate and follow you; misbehaving is no fun if no one is annoyed. If the dodging tactic persists, perhaps at exercise in an open space, it is perhaps because you have only called it to you when you mean to put the lead on and go – associated with the fun being over. Practise by calling back for praise and a pat, when there is more walk still to come. If this way does not work, then the dog must be put on to a very long rope, trailing behind it, and when it will not come tread on the end of the rope, and 'by magic' so far as the dog is concerned, pull it up short and haul the dog in rewarding it on arrival.

A puppy kept with an older dog is seldom

Above Some measure of control has been achieved. The dog is still playing up.

Right Learning not to get ahead of the handler. The newspaper held in front of the dog's head is a deterrent.

Far right Finally, the dog is manageable and under complete control, and both owner and dog can enjoy the walk.

Left This miniature
poodle is trimmed to
the lamb cut rather
than the lion cut
required for showing.
Above The shih tzu was
thought by Buddhists
to resemble a lion. The
head held proudly on a
strong neck is a feature
of the breed.
Right The lhasa apso
may have originated
from a cross of Tibetan
terriers and Tibetan
spaniels.

Weekly practice in
ringcraft in preparation
for showing.

troublesome about coming when called, if
one obeys the other will be quick to find out
what it is missing. Hunting breeds loose on
the scent of game are very often deaf to all
except their natural instincts. This is a
situation you have to assess and guard against
if you keep these breeds.

Never encourage a dog to jump up at you;
but rather get down to its level so that it may
greet you as it would other dogs. If you say
'Down!' mean it, and make the dog by force
of will, stay on all fours, but do remember
that it delights in your arrival and provide
your pet with some acceptable way to wel-
come you. Throw a ball and let the dog
bring it, or give it a glove to carry away,
and exhibit with pride to the household.
Our dogs used to greet us with wagging
rears, and toys held in their mouths which

we would take with elaborate thanks. It
served to distract them from knocking us
over. It does seem a pity to curb their joy
and exuberance. Some people keep an old
overall in the hall to slip on to protect town
clothes from doggy welcomes. If you want
to enjoy your dog to the full, then you will
invent your own remedies.

You should train your puppy from an
early age to wear a soft collar for short times
while supervised, but it should never be
left on when the puppy is alone. Lead
training should begin in the garden, and
then progress to the road. Never try to lead-
train a puppy when you are on an errand.
Make it a special job, a few minutes every
day of concentration until it is walking at
your side, without pulling forward or back.
Personally, I hate to see a pet dog walking to

68

heel. I like them at my side with no tension on the lead at all. Pulling on the lead gets more difficult to eradicate as the weeks go by. Nothing looks more foolish than an owner being towed along, whether by a tiny pug tugging away just in front, or a Dobermann at full gallop with the owner's feet scarcely touching the ground. Don't let it begin. Keep the lead short, and if the dog pulls forward, turn and go the other way until it is at your side once more. Then prevent the dog getting ahead either by waving a rolled newspaper in front of its nose, or control on the neck by a slip-lead or check-chain. A sharp tug can be felt by the dog and will register, but prolonged hauling on its neck will cause it to cough, salivate, and may cause injury. Persistence and practice when you are not in a hurry will convey your intentions, and you may congratulate yourself that you have taught your dog something which will serve you and it well all its days. Some pups that don't pull, may sit down and refuse to move at all. Patient encouragement and time spent is the answer, and possibly a trained dog to go with as example. Dogs can be taught good social behaviour at training classes, but few will accept pupils before five or six months, and the groundwork should have been done by then.

Always keep your dog on a short lead close by your side in the street. Do not let it approach other dogs or people unasked, and never speak to or let your dog interfere with a guide dog for the blind in harness which has to concentrate on its job.

One of the main reasons you bought your puppy was to enjoy play with it, but be careful not to overexcite, and when play-time is over, make the fact very clear, saying the same, simple word each time. The dog will learn to retire to its bed to sleep or watch your further moves. 'Bed!' is another useful command, but make sure that you are obeyed. 'Sit!' is taught by pushing down the puppy's hindquarters as you say the word. Just before mealtimes is a useful time to have some little dominating routine which it performs, just as control is gained over a horse by dressage movements. Sitting and giving a paw, or sitting, lying right down, and then standing is a good idea before the food bowl goes down. The dog will have its attention fixed on you when it sees dinner preparation anyway. Do not prolong the agony, however; one or two little tricks are enough. With the big breeds, insist on calm behaviour indoors always, because a boisterous bull mastiff can wreck a room in no time.

In training your dog, consistency in following a command through is the key-note. The dog must always do what you have said, even though you may begin to wish you had not said it, but it can only learn what it is taught. If when it misbehaves you shut it outside, and always confine it to the kitchen when visitors come, your dog will never learn to conduct itself with dignity. Naturally, you will be anxious to have your dog trained as soon as possible, but you should expect, as you would in a child, some attempts to test your firmness, and some times when no progress is made. Do not expect too much, too soon, remembering that the dog that always behaves perfectly is just as repressed as the child who is always good. It does an animal no harm to be ignored for periods of time, when you are busy at home. These are the times when no demands are made of the dog and it is allowed to be just a dog.

Any dog depends upon companionship and enjoys hearing you talk, but it also needs a balance of peace and quiet. Puppies must be allowed to sleep until they wake naturally, and should not be constantly disturbed by one member of the family after another wanting to exploit its attractiveness. When a puppy tires of play and seeks its bed, it is a good idea to leave it alone, even if only to go into another room. At first it should be accustomed to being alone for periods of ten minutes, increasing gradually to an hour-and-a-half at five months, and about three hours being reasonable for a fully trained adult. Refusal to stay alone indicates lack of training in first instance, or boredom and loneliness later. Many dogs react to boredom by doing damage to the home, for which you may be angry. You should direct your anger against yourself, however, if you have asked of the dog more than it is capable of enduring.

If you train the puppy to stay alone while you are still in the house, you can return at once if you hear the door being scratched, and intimate that this behaviour is not allowed. I would not expect a six-week-old puppy to stay alone in a strange kitchen for the first few nights that it is in your home; it is unreasonable to do so. The youngster has

These working Old
English sheepdogs are
helping their owner
round up cattle.

Icelandic dogs har-
nessed in a team
pulling a sledge, often
the only means of
transport across snowy
wastes.

left the warm, dog-smelling security of its litter and its breeder's home where all the rooms have the familiar scents, and the voices were those which were first heard. The day with you may have been fun, but when the puppy is left, it feels disoriented and lonely, its instinct suggests that it should not be alone, and it howls for the pack. The little dog may be silenced by repeated scolding, but it is not the beginning of a good, trusting relationship. You want this dog to love and respect you, to look to you for everything, to be always willing to come to you in the face of stress and danger. Opening the kitchen door and slapping the dog hard when it is frightened and lonely is not a good basis on which to start.

I ask the people who buy my puppies to forget their scruples and to take the puppy to bed with them for at least the first week of ownership. If they are very opposed to having the puppy on the bed, they must settle it down in a cardboard box beside them, where they can put out a comforting hand and speak kindly when it feels lonely and homesick. The dam will rush to her puppies when she hears the distress cry, and you will be carrying on this rôle and imprinting yourself on the puppy both as its provider and its pack leader who defends the weak. I am sure this provides the best beginning for a good and devoted dog/human relationship, and you will get a more obedient and compliant dog for life. There is also the advantage of day and night house training, because when the puppy stirs in the early hours you can take it out at once. The puppy need not sleep in the bedroom for more than about two weeks. By that time it will be thoroughly accustomed to you, your house and garden, and its new way of life. It will have learned the word 'No!' and the use of its bed downstairs in the daytime. At that stage you can insist that the dog stays in the kitchen at night, and although you may have to reinforce your commands several times it should not be frightened in addition to wanting your company. Many theories have been advanced for putting hot water bottles, furry toys, and ticking clocks in their beds to keep the puppies quiet. In my experience there is nothing like warm people for comforting lonely puppies. If you already have another dog or a cat, it would be expecting a lot to leave them alone together for the first week.

Allow the resident animal to accept the newcomer on his or her own terms gradually. All other aspects of training, such as not worrying at meals, walking on furniture, biting at shoe laces are within your own capacity for training now; you need only apply vigilance and the word 'No!' Expect obedience, but not to the extent of extinguishing the spirit of fun and spontaneous gaiety which the dog can bring to your life.

Your puppy will soon learn the bounds of good behaviour and will probably be very obedient until about the six to nine months' age of adolescence, when it will be trying itself for size and will openly defy you, in a bid for supremacy. Most powerful, large breed males need to have one or two confrontations with their owners at this stage, when they need to be strongly dominated to emphasize that they are not contenders for pack leadership. Pressing the head and back of neck to the ground, holding it down for a few minutes is what the pack leader would do, and using a growling voice is very effective, as is throwing something from a distance to hit the wall behind it, or shouting from a window where it did not expect you to be. The dog is easily impressed by the unexpected. In the bigger breeds a little fear of its master is not a bad thing in the strong-willed male that might otherwise develop such a strong character as would be uncontainable in a pet. This is a long way from the fear that brings cringeing and subjection; perhaps healthy respect would be a better word than fear. A thorough shaking, such as its canine peers would give the pup, is a more effective punishment than a deliberately inflicted beating, and far more useful than the swipe that misses him.

Dogs will sometimes be deliberately naughty, as a child will, to attract attention, and to see what they can get away with. My house dogs know that it is forbidden to rush at the wire to bark at kennelled dogs, yet they will often do it. I have noticed that if I do not stop them at once, they will hesitate and look over their shoulders at the house, just waiting for me to come out and break up the melee. They often put on this performance when visitors are present, perhaps with the idea of breaking up the tea party so that they can sneak back and finish the biscuits. We have never had completely well-behaved dogs; we try to have fun dogs that are not a nuisance to themselves or to other people.

showing dogs

SHOWING IN BRITAIN

We do not know when the first dog show was held, but probably pride in the ownership of a beautiful or clever animal will always have led to comparing one dog with another, and asking a third person which is the best, which in essence, is what showing amounts to. Until The Kennel Club was formed in 1873, dog shows in Britain were hampered by many controversial rules, and much faking went on, because there was no supervising body to hold records. The Kennel Club was not accepted by everyone when it was first convened, but it gradually came to preside over all dog registration and exhibition, as it does today. The most important task of The Kennel Club is to hold the standards for each breed, the specification of height, colour, coat texture, and so on which makes each breed what it is.

In showing a dog we are offering for the judge's approval what we think is as close as possible to The Kennel Club standard for the breed. The judge picks what he or she thinks are the best animals; those which in the judge's opinion most nearly satisfy the requirements of the breed standard as he/she interprets it. It is this personal interpretation which makes showing interesting, and makes it possible for a dog to be a big winner on one day and quite ignored the next. Breed standards are amended from time to time by a committee from clubs for the breeds. Thus, breeds develop and change in type slightly over the years. The Kennel Club has also organized the registration of dogs, so that each dog has only one name. Before registration was introduced it was not unheard of for a dog to appear under several different names. The Kennel Club also keeps records of a dog's wins so that unfair

Judging the bulldogs at the Ladies' Kennel Association, Holland House, Kensington, London 1896.

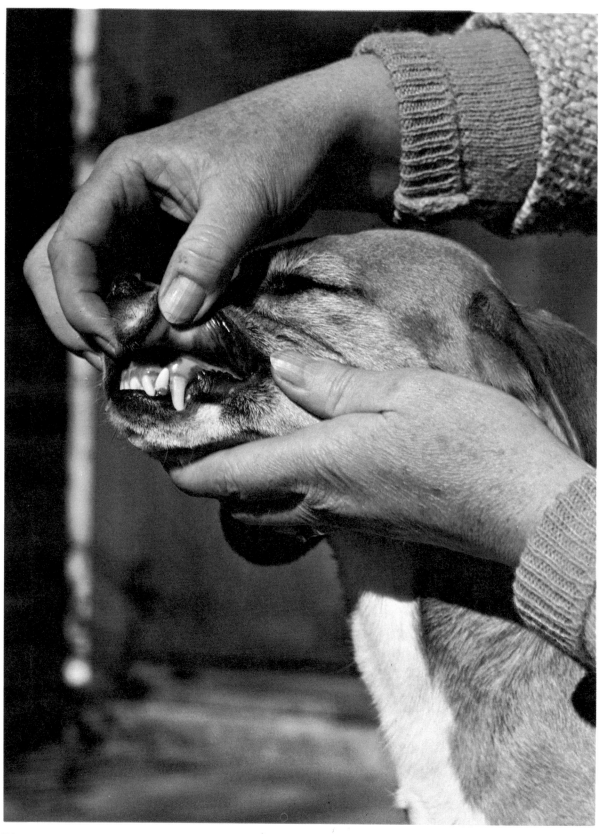

Regular inspection of teeth and gums can prevent pain and loss of appetite in the ageing dog.

Above A sponge-down for the large, short-coated dog.

Right This Pekingese is being trained from puppy days to enjoy its daily grooming session.

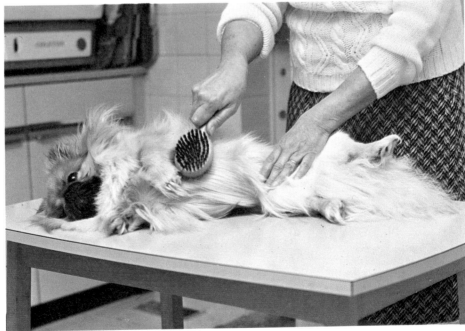

competition is not possible. A dog will be quickly disqualified from its wins if they are ones for which it was ineligible. All dog shows and club matches must be licensed by The Kennel Club, and held according to Kennel Club rules.

During the latter half of the 1800s and the beginning of the 1900s dog breeding was a very popular hobby of the British aristocracy and landed gentry. Queen Victoria had an extensive kennel in which she took great personal interest, although she mixed her breeds together with cheerful abandon and kept some very atypical specimens. Beautiful and unusual dogs were favourite presents between visiting royal families. The intermarriage of the royal siblings meant that many new types of dog came into the royal kennels first. The new breed would become very exclusive, puppies being given only to favoured friends. The origin of the dog would be a status symbol.

During the first decade of the 1900s it was customary to send dogs alone to dog shows, by rail or carrier. The dogs would remain there for two or three days, during which time they were attended by kennel staff provided by the show management. Animals would be fed by food manufacturers to advertise their products. With increasing awareness of personal responsibility for our dogs, these practices would be quite unacceptable now. All dogs must be accompanied at all times to shows. It is only with the innovation of modern protective vaccines that showing has become totally safe. Not many decades ago, exhibitors had to be prepared to lose a winning dog through distemper caught at a show, and perhaps to have the disease spread throughout their kennels. Even now it is possible to contract viral infections, such as kennel cough, where dogs are crowded together in dusty conditions, but considering the number of dogs gathered together, shows are remarkably disease free. In fact, compulsory veterinary inspection at the entrance has now been dispensed with for some years. There is always veterinary help available if necessary, and at some shows random checks are made to ensure that no dogs suffering from infectious conditions are present.

The Princess of Wales, later to be Queen Alexandra Consort to Edward VII, did much to make dog breeding popular among wealthy Edwardian ladies, who were quick to copy the fashions of the Royal Family. The ladies wanted to attend dog shows too, but they found that going to the regular shows, being justled by men, and seeing them take alcoholic drink in public, was just too much to bear. The ladies sought to run their own shows, under The Kennel Club, at which only dogs owned by women could be exhibited. The Ladies' Kennel Association was founded in 1894; it was soon noticed how many winning dogs were transferred from husband to wife! The prizes at the ladies' shows were very enviable, including silver bracelets, tea sets, and dressing table sets, in addition to challenge cups. These shows were very fashionable occasions, and as well as very frank commentary on the dogs, far more outspoken than would be tolerated today, the *Ladies' Kennel Gazette* carried descriptions of the ladies' toilettes and parasols. Their dogs were sometimes decorated to match, and the prize rosettes were sometimes ordered in tones to suit the dress of the lady expected to win. The quality of dogs in the ladies' kennels was quite high, because the dogs were actually in the hands of grooms and stablemen who were quite ruthless in their selection of stock.

After World War I interest in dogs was shown by a different public composed largely of the ex-officers who invested their gratuities in smallholdings. Dog owning spread to the middle classes; dogs began to be bred in private homes instead of the stables and kennels of mansions, but the breeding involved more sentiment and less selection. Today, dog showing and breeding is completely classless; entries are huge and the competition is very keen. Improved transport methods mean that an ambitious owner can go to the shows far from home, so that competition is no longer regional. Dogs entering Britain from other countries must go through six months' quarantine. In practice, this means that British owners are not able to show dogs in Europe or the United States and easily bring them back again. International champions must have been made up in two different countries. It is possible to do this in Britain by qualifying a dog in Eire in addition to its mainland title.

Cruft's Dog Show is well known throughout the showing world. Charles Cruft was a dog biscuit salesman turned entrepreneur, whose name is synonymous with the dog show. He held his first show in 1886, just four years after the formation of The Kennel Club. By 1891 Cruft's Show was an annual event at the Agricultural Hall at Islington, London, where it was held until 1939. It is a great thing among dog exhibitors to have been at a Cruft's at the Agricultural Hall. Dog shows were suspended during World War II, except on a very regional basis. After Charles Cruft's death, his widow sold the goodwill of the show to The Kennel Club, which has run it as the Club's show, at Olympia, London since 1948. Even though it is held at the beginning of February, in some of the worst of British weather, this show has a special attraction and many overseas visitors come to see British stock, which they hope to buy.

Many British visitors come to this show too, far more than we ever see at shows which are held in more pleasant surroundings, at better times, and with additional attractions. Cruft's is the mecca of all dog exhibitors. Entries became so huge that in latter years it has been necessary for dogs to qualify for Cruft's by winning specific prizes at other shows; the qualifications vary slightly from year to year, and have had the desired effect of eliminating the purely pet quality dogs which were often entered solely for the glory of saying, 'It was at Cruft's,' although standing not a chance of a prize.

It may be that you have bought your puppy with an idea of making dog showing your hobby, or perhaps that at the training class someone knowledgeable has told you that the dog is good enough to show. It would still be as well to contact the breeder, if possible, for a specialist opinion. Most breeders are delighted to have their stock go into the show ring, but rather dismayed if you insist on exhibiting an animal which was sold only as pet quality, or has not turned out according to early promise. Go to one or two shows without your dog, to gain the idea of the show specimen, and the feel of the atmosphere, before you and the dog begin in the competition together, when you are bound to feel tense and nervous.

Before you can show the dog it must be registered at The Kennel Club and transferred into your name. If the dog's papers have not been returned by the time you make your show entry, you must put NAF (name applied for) or TAF (transfer applied for) after its name. If the dog is held in partnership, or on breeding terms, then the actual owners must sign the show entry form. You should then take your dog to a ringcraft or training class, so that you will not be embarrassed by a badly shown animal. It is a complete waste of time and money to take a dog to a show if it will not stand, move, and pose, and allow the judge to handle it. You will find that the other exhibitors are expert in presentation. Your dog must learn to concentrate on its job, even with the distraction of other dogs, people, and the noise of loudspeakers and applause. You have to learn to subdue your own nerves, and to present the dog so that its virtues are obvious and its faults are as hidden as possible. If you can find a ringcraft class at your local canine society, you will be taught just what to do, and you will be made aware of local shows. If the training class is only in obedience, do not put too much emphasis on the 'sit' command, if you mean to show the dog in beauty competition, because sitting is very undesirable; in the show ring, dogs are always viewed standing, and in profile.

There are four main types of dog show in Britain: *the beauty show*, concentrating on breed conformation and looks; *the obedience competition*, in which a dog and its owner carry out a set pattern of orders, and are judged on the accuracy with which they obey. Competition is very keen, often only half a point separating the winners, and a crooked sit can lose you marks. German shepherd dogs, border collies, and Labradors excel at obedience work, but owners of notoriously difficult breeds enjoy the challenge of this type of competition. A dog may become an obedience champion and a show champion by working in both types of competition; *field trial competitions* are for gundogs, involving retrieving work on land and water with both animals and birds. The ultimate accolade is field trial champion, which may also be a beauty champion; *working trials* are in some ways similar to obedience tests, but they involve greater use of initiative on the part of the dog, and a more strenuous performance. The title of companion dog (CD) with the grading 'Excellent' involves an agility test of long jump and high jump as well as the more ordinary obedience actions.

Above **A summer show where the dogs are benched in marquees.** *Left* **The judge is assessing these Pyrenean mountain dogs for strength of back and bone conformation.** *Right* **Judging in progress in several rings at a large championship show.**

The utility dog stake includes scenting and ground search. The dog will hope to qualify UD (Ex). The working dog competition becomes even more difficult with retrieval of a stranger's lost articles; a winner will be labelled WD (Ex). A tracking dog must follow a track half a mile long and three hours cold successfully, in addition to the other tests. The police dog stake will normally only be entered by dogs owned by professional handlers, because it involves pursuit and detention of a running human being acting as a 'criminal'. It would be most unwise to encourage a family pet to undertake this sort of work. Any of the working trial awards are difficult to win and show great co-operation between handler and dog. While it is more usual to compete with the large breeds, tiny dogs also make a gallant show, the jumps being scaled down to their size.

THE BEAUTY SHOW

Beauty showing is by far the most popular, and there is a wide range of types of show, and many opportunities to be at a show every week. Beginners are often advised to make their first efforts at an *Exemption Show*, which is a show that has been granted a licence to be exempt from the usual Kennel Club rules. Such shows are often held in conjunction with flower shows and fêtes. They have as many as four classes for pedigree dogs, which need not be Kennel Club registered, and then further novelty classes for 'longest wagging tail' and so on. Entries at this show may be made on the day, so that you can take part on impulse. In fact, the competition may be very hard indeed, with huge classes of animals of many breeds, and a hardpressed judge who has not always had very wide experience of the many breeds of dogs. A good animal may sometimes be overlooked, and a promising exhibitor be discouraged. The same thing may happen at Club matches, where dogs drawn at random from the entry are matched one against another. Two good dogs coming up against each other in the first round inevitably result in one being knocked out. Your best method of entry into showing is at a Limited, Sanction, or Open Show, having classes for your breed. The Limited and Sanction Shows restrict the number of classes, and the amount of wins the dogs have had up to

the time of entry. The Open Show is open to all-comers. If you enter in breed classes, you will be comparing your dog with its own kind, under a specialist judge, and you are likely to get help and opinions from other people who have been showing the breed longer than you. You will find their attitude very generous to a beginner, you will be shown what to do, and get advice on presenting your dog, if you ask for it. Before going into the ring, most beginners are very nervous, but you will probably forget about your nerves, once you are trying to show your dog to the best advantage. Many people have conquered nerves and agoraphobia by attending dog shows. In Britain advance notices of the beauty shows appear in the two weekly papers of the fancy, *Dog World* and *Our Dogs*. Once you become interested in showing, you will want to subscribe to these papers, because they contain specialized notes about the breeds, and also the judges' reports on the first three winners in each class they judge. If your dog was 'placed' you will be anxious to discover what sort of a 'write-up' it was given – you will be learning a whole new vocabulary too!

For your first showing year, you will have to write to each show management for a schedule of the show they are advertising. The following year they should arrive automatically, if you have once made an entry. The schedule will tell you what classes are available, who is judging them, the cost of the entry, and car park and so on. It may also include a map of the venue and details of catering arrangements. Club shows restrict the entry to membership of the club, but you can always join when you enter. You will find that entries have to be received by a certain date, perhaps six weeks ahead of the show, so that the catalogue can be printed to include details of the breeding of each exhibit. The closing date means what it says, and late entries will be rejected. In classes such as Novice, which is restricted to dogs that have only won a limited amount of prizes, you may have to delay your entry until the last minute, if you are attending other shows with the opportunity to 'win yourself out of Novice'. In such a case it is as well to obtain proof of sending your entry before the closing date. Exhibitors' passes should reach you before the day of the show. If they do not, and you have proof of your entry, you can go along and be allowed to

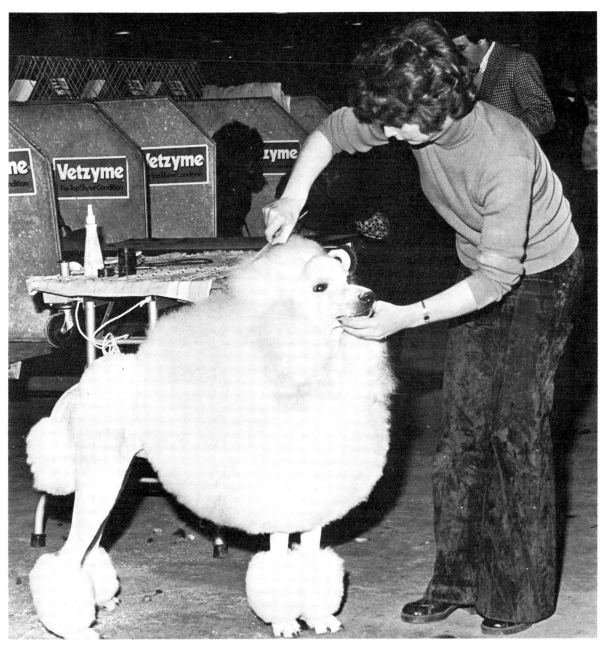

The final touches before Springett Trillium in the Park, a standard poodle in show trim, goes into the ring.

compete. You will find in the schedule printed definitions of the classes, so that you may deduce which gives your dog the best chance. Puppy and Junior are restricted by age, and a new dog, if well grown, stands a chance of meeting its equals. Novice class may contain quite mature dogs which for some reason have not been shown very much. You need not attend a show for which you have entered but if your dog is there, then it must appear in each class for which you have entered it, unless specially excused by

reason of illness. Even if you are quite out of the running, you must appear in each class – perhaps a good reason for not making too big an entry the first few times.

At the big Open and Championship Shows, the dogs will be 'benched' – that is, provided with individual compartments or cages, where they must spend their time when not in the show ring, or exercising for short periods. You must remain at these shows until the advertised time of departure, which is usually late in the afternoon, so that

Terrier expert
trimming out a West
Highland white terrier

the public may have a chance to see the dogs. In most cases, you will want to remain beside your dog, because it will be worried by the new experience. In any case, you can learn much by seeing and being seen on the show benches, rather than looking at the trade stands. At unbenched shows dogs are tied to radiators or under the chairs, and are made as comfortable as possible. They may also be left in cars, if the weather is not too hot, and only brought out when their class is ready to go on. At such shows there can be little restriction for leaving after your classes.

When you have been at dog shows as a member of the public, without your dog, you will have noted the accepted show presentation for your breed. There is little purpose in taking a pet dog straight from your home to compete with dogs that are worked on daily to keep them in show trim.

Of course, the dog's coat, ears, and eyes must be clean anyway, but many breeds have a particular show trim, or length of coat about which only a specialist of the breed can advise you. If you have been to a ringcraft class, then this advice is likely to be available there. For some breeds, particularly terriers and larger working dogs, some owners employ professional handlers, who will, for a fee, put the dog's coat in order, and present the animal in the ring to the best advantage. It may even be necessary for the dog to live with the handler and be brought to the shows by him or her, so that the owner reaps little beyond the glory and the expense. While a professional handler can certainly make the best of a dog, it is more satisfying to feel that you and your dog owe what success you have to your mutual co-operation.

On the day, the show judge's methods

and opinions are the only ones that count. Judges are chosen by the show committee, and they may be breed specialists, or one of the well-known all-rounders, who have had experience in a group of breeds or many breeds. When you have been showing for a while, you will learn to play your judges, to know which one is particular about correct mouths, or will only put up small animals, or ones of a particular colour. The judge is looking for the dogs which most nearly approximate to his/her interpretation of the breed standard. Most of the standards give plenty of scope for a personal viewpoint, and some judges will put all-round soundness as their most important features before colour or size, for example. There are four prize cards in each class: First, Second, Third, and Reserve; there may also be a Very Highly Commended card. Money prizes are usually given with the first three places and sometimes there are rosettes, and special prizes and cups. The colours of prize cards are always the same: red First, blue Second, yellow Third, and green Reserve; white is Very Highly Commended. The coveted Challenge Certificate, offered for the best of each sex at a Championship Show, is white edged with green and is often called the 'green card' or 'the ticket'. Three of these, given by three different judges, make a dog a champion, and there is no limit to the number a dog may win, provided they are under different judges. It is considered very bad form to enter your dog again under a judge who has awarded it a challenge certificate once, because it puts the judge in an embarrassing position, and may prevent another dog gaining a certificate it deserves.

When you take your groomed and exercised dog into the ring, you will find there one or more stewards, whose job it is to organize the ring for the judge, write up the awards' board, and give out the ring numbers. You must be ready to quote your number from the catalogue, and have a safety pin or badge ready to pin this ring number prominently on your person, so that those at the ringside can refer to the breeding particulars in the catalogue, and note down the place you are awarded. You will probably be asked to lead your dog round in a circle with the others, so that the judge can make a preliminary assessment of movement. Dogs should be on the inside of the ring. The judge wants to see your dog.

Then the judge will stop the parade, and examine each dog individually, small dogs on a table, larger ones in the centre of the ring. Your dog must be accustomed to being handled by strangers, having its mouth opened, and the male to having his testicles felt to see if both are in the scrotum. A unilateral cryptorchid dog may be shown, but under many judges it would need to be a particularly fine animal before it would be considered for a prize. A spayed bitch may not be exhibited unless she has had a litter which has already been registered at The Kennel Club. A male that has had a vasectomy cannot be shown either. When the judge asks to see the dog's mouth it is the bite and teeth that are to be inspected, not its tonsils; you just curl up the dog's lips so that the teeth are revealed. You will then be asked to move your dog individually. Listen to the judge, and don't get flustered. Some judges like the dog to move in a straight line, some in a triangle. Take a minute to prepare your dog ready for moving, especially if it has just been lifted from the table. Then move at the pace you have practised, taking care that the dog does not jump up at you or break into a gallop. Most judges will give you a second chance to move if you spoil it the first time. Do try not to lose your sense of direction in the ring, and come straight back towards the judge, who will be looking for correct movement of the dog's front legs, which cannot be seen from an angle. You will then have a moment to relax, while the rest of the dogs are moved, but when the judge is watching the last dog, begin to pose yours, so that his or her eye may fall on a perfect silhouette when glancing around the ring again. You will doubtless have been shown how to have some titbit, or toy in your pocket, or your hand, to keep the dog's head at the angle you want, or to keep its tail wagging in anticipation. You rather tantalize the dog with this titbit, because it is not correct to feed the dog in the ring, nor is it favoured to do anything which may distract another dog. In Britain it is very much forbidden to have anyone at the ringside to attract your dog, and you will be warned by the stewards if found doing this.

In a big class the judge may pick out a quantity of hopefuls, asking them to congregate in the middle of the ring, for another selection to be made. In this case the others will quietly leave the ring. In smaller classes the judge will pick out the five placings, but the order may be reversed until the moment the card is in your hand, and you should never give up. Prize money is paid at the show, where it may be pinned to the award card, or at the big Championship Shows the cards have a tear-off section which you take to the treasurer's tent. Do remember to collect your money, and any cups for which you have qualified. If you win your class, wait quietly by the ringside, because you may be called in with other winners to compete for Best Puppy, Best Dog, or Best Bitch. At Championship Shows the Challenge Certificate winner is not by any means always the winner of the Open class; it may come in to challenge from the winners of a lower class, even Puppy. The winners of each sex then meet each other for Best of Breed. At an Open Show, the best of each breed then meets the best of each other breed scheduled (and the Variety class winners) under a different judge, who decides Best in Show. At large Championship Shows, which often extend to three days, the second round of judging is by groups, the Best of Breed winner meeting all others in its group, that is, the toy dogs, the gundogs, or terriers, and so on. From these group winners, an ultimate winner is chosen for the overall Best in Show – it is a very great honour indeed, for both the dog and the person asked to judge it.

Whether your dog has won a prize or not you may feel that you would like to know the judge's opinion. It is helpful to know if there is any future in showing for it, or whether you should, with more insight, buy a second dog to show, as so many people do. Most judges will be happy to tell you what they think, provided you ask tactfully at the right time. If judging has finished early and the judge is not examining another breed, it may be that he or she will come to the benches, and answer any questions then, and it is as well to be available. Otherwise, wait until the end of the judging, until the cups are presented and the photographs taken and then make your approach politely. You may also be given useful hints and encouragement, particularly on presentation, an important aspect of showing.

The Junior Warrant is a Kennel Club award, given to young dogs which amass a total of twenty-one points for show wins, before they are eighteen months old. This award may be mentioned on the pedigree of the dog, but it does not help in its qualification to be a Champion. Entry in the Stud Book is an honour confined to dogs and bitches winning Challenge Certificates, and First, Second, or Third in the top classes at Championship Shows. The animal is then awarded a new number, instead of its puppy registration number, and you will use this Stud Book number with pride thereafter. The entry will appear in that year's Kennel Club Stud Book, and it means that your dog is noted for ever in the Kennel Club hierarchy as one of the leading animals of its day. Kennel Club Stud Books are issued free to Associates of the Kennel Club, or may be purchased. Secondhand copies have some rarity value because they are collected by people keen on tracing pedigrees for many generations.

You can travel to the show by car or by rail. Rail is popular for long distances, when the management will probably have arranged for buses to convey you from the station to the show ground. You will also find in the dog papers advertisements for privately organized coach trips, on which you can book a double seat for yourself and dog, at a very moderate price. You can learn a lot about dog showing on one of these trips. You should be equipped with your grooming kit, towels, benching rug and chain, a bottle of water and bowl (dogs often dislike water from a different source) ice for the short-faced breeds, food for yourself and your dogs, your passes, and a pencil. Do not take too much money with you because unfortunately thieves find exhibitors' preoccupation with their dogs an excellent opportunity. Dogs are not usually fed until after they have been in the ring, unless your animal is slab-sided and looks better with a rounded abdomen. When you are deciding what to wear, remember that the spectators will have a constant view of you from the back, bending down! Most exhibitors like to use garments with pockets for their combs and pieces of liver, but overalls have never caught on although they would seem to be so suitable. You may like to plan your outfit with a view to finding the ideal colour against which to pose your dog. Even if the sun is blazing down, take all your wet weather equipment, for whatever happens, the show goes on.

SHOWING ON THE CONTINENT

Showing in most countries on the continent is conducted according to the rules laid down by the international body, the *Fédération Cynologique Internationale* (*FCI*) which has its headquarters in Belgium.

In general there are fewer classes allocated to each breed than in Britain, with working dogs and field trial classes where appropriate. All dogs have to be at least nine months old before they can be entered at a show. Judges grade each exhibit, according to merit, Excellent, Very Good, Good, Satisfactory, Unsatisfactory. Excellent is only given to outstanding dogs and is not usually awarded to any under the age of two years unless they are of exceptional quality. Strong emphasis is placed on dentition, some countries disqualifying dogs which do not have all their teeth present, and others giveing the dog a lower grade.

Two types of certificates are awarded: the national certificate, *Certificat d'Aptitude au Championat* (*CAC*), and the international, *Certificat d'Aptitude au Championat International de Beauté* (*CACIB*). The former is equivalent to our Challenge Certificate and counts towards the title of Champion in the country where the dog competes. The latter is only awarded at shows designated *Internationale*.

The rules governing the award of the title National Champion differ slightly from country to country. The usual number of CACs required is four under four different judges, although at shows, such as a Breed Championship Show, or in Holland, the annual Winners Show, a CAC counts for two. Other requirements may be for a CAC to be won at a specific show held only once a year, to be won after the age of two years, or for at least a year to have elapsed between the award of the first and last CAC.

In order to become an international champion a dog must be awarded four CACIBs in not less than three different countries under three different judges. If both CACs and CACIBs are available at the same show, the judge may award the CAC but withold the CACIB if he or she does not consider the exhibit to be worthy of the title International Champion. There is usually a lower age limit below which a dog may not be awarded a CACIB or CAC.

SHOWING IN SCANDINAVIA

The Scandinavian system differs slightly from both the British and continental ones. Two classes are scheduled, Junior, eight to fifteen months, and Open, over fifteen months. In these two classes a dog is not graded but is given a First, Second or Third prize, or a o if it is a very poor specimen. In theory, it would be possible to have a class consisting entirely of First prize winners if all the exhibits were good enough and, conversely, if the quality is poor, no dog need be given a prize. From the First prize winners the best four are chosen in both Junior and Senior classes, and from the winners of the Senior classes come the Certificate winners.

SHOWING IN EIRE

A 'Green Star' points system operates in the Republic of Ireland (Eire) and the number of points awarded depends on the number of dogs present in the arena on the day, as in the American system. There is no quarantine restriction between the mainland of Britain and the Republic of Ireland or the Channel Islands.

SHOWING IN THE UNITED STATES OF AMERICA

In the United States where there is a flourishing dog fancy the system whereby a dog becomes a Champion is quite different from that described above, and is on a points basis. Five classes for both sexes are scheduled: Puppy, Novice, Bred-by-exhibitor, American-bred, and Open (imported dogs may only compete in this class). There are two other classes: Winner's Dog and Winner's Bitch in which the winners of the five previous classes compete, and from these the best dog and bitch, the Points Winners, are chosen. The number of points is calculated according to the number of eligible dogs competing in the regular classes of each sex in each breed or variety. These then compete for Best of Winners and finally both of them go forward to the Best of Breed class in which Champions are entered.

A dog becomes a Champion when it has won fifteen points, and a Champion of Record 'if six or more of said points shall have been won at two shows with a rating of three or more championship points each and under two different judges, and some one or more of the balance of said points shall have been won under some other judge or judges than the two judges referred to above'. (American Kennel Club [AKC] rules apply to registration and showing.)

A strong criticism of American and similar systems is that dogs which are competing for the title of Champion never have to come up against established Champions. Once a dog achieves its title, it is restricted to the Best of Breed class. As in Britain there are group winners and an eventual Best in Show.

AKC regulations make it mandatory for judges to 'excuse' from the ring any dog which growls or attempts to bite the judge, or which is lame. The reason for this excusal is entered on the judging slip.

SHOWING IN AUSTRALIA

Basically, Australian regulations are the same throughout the country, but there are some differences between States in the conduct of shows and the award of the title of Champion. Each of the seven States has its own kennel club which is responsible for all administration within that State. The Australian National Kennel Club holds meetings of State kennel club delegates a few times each year. Its function, however, is purely advisory and its recommendations do not have to be taken into State practice. There is no strong, central co-ordinating body and there would seem to be an urgent need for the formation of a governing national club.

The requirements for making up an Australian champion differ considerably from those in Britain, being on a points basis and with young puppies of three months or over being shown. The Winner of the Points is chosen from the class winners, including puppies of six months and over. For the Challenge Certificate a dog earns five points plus an additional point for each competing dog over the age of six months up to a maximum of twenty-five points. Groups and Best in Show are judged in a similar manner to Britain and the group winner receives twenty-five points to count towards the title of Australian Champion, for which a total of 100 points is necessary.

OTHER RULES AND REGULATIONS

Many countries place much importance on the preservation of working qualities in dogs and make it a condition that champions must have a qualification in this. In Russia, it is understood that an obedience diploma is needed before a dog may be shown in beauty classes. Toy dogs must carry out basic obedience tests (sit, down, and stay) gun dogs field tests, and guard dogs attack work.

In Germany, after passing a test of suitability for breeding, which requires a certain standard of conformation and temperament, a dog or bitch may only qualify for entry in the Stud Book if it has been given the grading of Excellent or Very Good by two judges of the breed, as well as having the minimum working qualification of SchH 1 and being the sire of progeny with no serious faults.

Another major difference between British shows and those of many other countries is that to officiate as a judge in Britain it is not necessary to pass any test. In countries such as Germany, Holland, and Scandinavia, before a judge is considered to be capable of awarding certificates, he or she is required to undergo some form of training with an examination or assessment at the end. This training may take the form of formal lectures on anatomy and veterinary subjects, followed by a written examination, and/or a period of apprenticeship as an aspiring judge. Before being accepted as an apprentice in Germany, the would-be judge has to have been a breeder of good stock for at least five years, to have no civil convictions, and must write a paper on some aspect of a chosen breed. After that the candidate attends five or six shows in attendance on a senior judge who carries out the actual judging and discusses the dogs with the apprentice. The apprentice has to write reports on all the dogs which are considered by the judges' panel of the breed club, together with a report from the senior judge or judges who have tutored him or her, at the end of the apprenticeship period. This panel makes the decision as to whether he or she is fit to judge a show. This seems an extremely sensible outlook and one which, it is felt, other kennel clubs, including The Kennel Club could emulate with advantage.

Breeding

When your puppy has grown to adulthood, you may want to consider the possibility of breeding from it. For the male pet dog the chances of being used at stud are very slim. Indeed, I should advise against allowing him to be used, unless you mean to turn him into a professional stud dog, and know that there will be a good number of bitches wishing to make use of his services. Demand for his use is only likely to come if he has won at shows, or if his own breeder wants his particular blood for a family line. Stud work is taught from about ten months old, and it inevitably makes a male more full of himself, more aggressive, and more inclined to wandering and territory marking. The professional stud settles to his work and does only what he should when necessary, but the dog which is only occasionally used is likely to be temperamentally disturbed.

Stud work does not quieten an unruly young animal. Most young males go through a stage of sexual awareness at about one year old when they seem acutely aware of the mating drive and will attempt ritual coupling with people or objects. This is probably due to hormone imbalance at the time. Such behaviour should be curbed as you do any other action that is not permitted, and the urge subsides with natural hormone adjustment. If the dog has an excessive or objectionable amount of libido beyond adolescence, then your veterinary surgeon can advise you about having him castrated.

Breeding from your bitch is a matter to consider when she is over one year old, and has had at least one season, more for slow maturing large breeds. There is no need to breed; the myth that every bitch needs a litter has long ago been proved wrong. Reproduction can bring as many uterine complications as can lifelong virginity or neutrality. You are not doing anything to ensure the bitch's healthy old age by breeding from her. Breeding takes time, money, space, and expertise. It brings work and worry, and you are very unlikely to profit financially. The pet bitch leads a most happy life after hysterectomy, or you may,

if you take care, see her through to old age having regular heat periods. The normal bitch continues to come into season until she dies. The spayed bitch need not get fat, as so many owners fear. She will have less stress to contend with, and more of her food will be deposited as fat, so that you should reduce her rations, or increase her exercise.

Never mate a bitch simply to make money. A litter is a gamble even for those who have been in the dog business a long time. For the beginner who means to do things properly, a litter will almost always mean financial loss. The breeder who takes the hobby seriously has invested in equipment, knowledge and reputation, had show wins, and probably does nothing but dogs in spare time. You will have a good deal of outlay on your first litter, and at first you will lack the expertise and contacts. It is also important to remember that you will have little advice to offer to the purchasers of your puppies, and no facilities to take them back should they become unwanted for any reason. You must also be aware that the bitch will almost certainly need someone present and some assistance at the birth, and if you are squeamish you should not try dog breeding.

There is always the temptation to breed and sell the litter to the many dealers who advertise for pedigree pups, for whom they have good homes waiting. The good homes are not necessarily domestic ones; they may be research laboratories, and they may not be in the country of the pup's birth. If you will care so little about the fate of the puppies you have raised that you do not want to know the homes they are to go to, please do not breed dogs, or any other animal. Any litter must be bred on the basis of keeping the pups until they can be sold individually with as much investigation of the purchaser as you are able to make. Having disposed of dog breeding as a way of making money, or as health insurance for the bitch, the only valid reason for breeding is to develop an improved dog to show, or to have a son or daughter to carry on from a beloved bitch. Even with such worthy reasons, you still have a lot of consideration to give. You must have time, and space.

Puppies need four months from conception to selling time. For most of this period you must be available, and holidays are out of the question for the last three months. Remember that you will be very lucky if all the pups sell as soon as they are eight weeks old. Even well-established breeders in Britain find that it is particularly difficult to sell during June, July, and August. Pups may not sell until the holidays are over. Dedicated breeders will refuse to sell at Christmas time, so that even if you mean to breed, careful calculation is needed when your bitch comes into season to make sure that you have allowed enough free time. Few boarding kennels will take a bitch in late pregnancy or a bitch with young puppies. Once you have set the whelping sequence into motion you must be prepared to carry it through without a holiday. It is a very serious undertaking. You need space, including a secluded room for the whelping, an indoor area large enough for the puppies when they start to run about, and some outside exercise. It is as well to know what is the maximum litter size for your breed and work to that, unless you are brave enough to cull the litter to the size you want. Then, you have to be sure of a market for your puppies. Study your local newspapers, and if there are several advertisements for pups of your breed week after week, it could be that the district is saturated. Many pet owners have been misled by promises from friends or relations to buy puppies, only to find they have unimpeachable reasons why they cannot oblige when the pups are ready.

Having tried to deter you from dog breeding for the wrong reasons, I am now glad to admit that watching over a birth and rearing pups is a most rewarding and exciting experience. For children of the right age it is a practical lesson in biology, an opportunity to get close to nature in an increasingly artificial world, and a unique chance to practise caring for a helpless creature that grows to independence much more quickly than the human baby. The snag is, the disposal of the surplus pups. In Britain, since 1 April 1974, if you have more than two bitches from which you mean to breed pups for sale, even with no profit involved, you must apply to your local authority for a licence under the Breeding of Dogs Act, which will mean that your premises must always be open to inspection by the public health authority, or their appointed agents. The licence is renewable yearly. The criteria for inspection vary, but generally refer to the number of dogs kept on the land available, adequate premises for whelping and care of puppies, food, heat, light, and fire precautions.

All dogs have a pedigree, as do all people. The difference between the mongrel and what we refer to as 'a pedigreed dog' is that in the latter case like has been bred to like and the names recorded, perhaps at The Kennel Club, and certainly by the breeder. The pedigree only has value in the strength of the names upon it, and the ability of those dogs to pass on their virtues. The much boasted of 'long as your arm' pedigree is just so much spoiled paper.

A pedigree with one or two predominant prefixes or affixes – as registered kennel names are termed – will mean that an owner has line bred, and will have personally known those dogs, or can certainly show you photographs of them. He or she will have aimed to keep or develop a special feature, type or strain within the breed specification of the dog. A pedigree containing in red ink the names of show winners or champions will mean that many people will know them. The pedigree containing a string of mixed or unknown names has little worth, because it does not help you to know anything of the background of your dog. Joining your breed club, buying the books on the breed, and meeting show breeders can all help you to explore the pedigree until it means something to you. It is also very helpful to meet through the breeder of your bitch her litter brothers and sisters in other ownership. Yours may have been the only beauty, or the only poor quality member of the litter, the one that remained small, or the only one with correct coat. Your bitch will have within her genetic make-up factors for most of the characteristics exhibited by her parents and her brothers and sisters. Without this knowledge you have little to guide you when choosing a sire for the pups.

Before you go any further with breeding plans, make sure that your bitch is registered at The Kennel Club, and transferred into your name. The only exception to this will be if you have obtained your bitch 'on breeding terms' agreement, whereby the breeder has control of the bitch until you have worked off some or all of the purchase price by the return of one or more puppies. If this agreement was not made legally binding and registered at The Kennel Club when you had the puppy, make sure that all is in order before you breed. The salient points are which party chooses the stud and pays the fee, who has the bitch for whelping, how many puppies go back to the breeder, in what order of choice, at what age the choice is to be made, and who is to register the puppies. Provision should also be made in case there are not enough puppies reared to satisfy the commitment. There is a great temptation to take a bitch pup 'on breeding terms' because it saves initial outlay, you are guided every step of the way with your litter, and you have some of the pups already booked. In cases of rare or very good show-winning bitches, it may be the only way to get the pup you want. On the other hand, breeding terms agreements often lead to dissatisfaction on one side or the other, and it is more rewarding to have freedom of action with the pups you have reared.

You will know that your bitch has qualities contributed by her parents, grand-parents, and those before them. Most of her attributes are hereditary, resulting from genes supplied by her sire and dam. If she has been 'line bred', that is, from reasonably related dogs over a number of years, a degree of relationship akin to human cousins, then even within her breed she will have recognizable qualities and she is likely to produce offspring of the same type. Much closer breeding, father to daughter, nephew to aunt, is a gambling business, only to be undertaken under the aegis of those who know the dogs and know what they are likely to get. You will be doubling up closely on all the virtues and vices, the tendencies to strength and weakness. You may get something very good and in the same litter a physical and mental aberration, or they may all be mediocre. I once mated aunt to nephew and discovered that there was epilepsy in the line which inbreeding brought out and made dominant. Some breeders do deliberate test matings, keeping all the pups to prove whether they have hip dysplasia, heart disease, or eye defects, and so on.

You must have your bitch examined by your vet, and tested for any of the hereditary diseases of the breed. You have the right to expect that a dog at public stud will also have been tested for physical fitness. It is not forbidden in Britain to breed from dogs with evidence of some disease, and indeed in some breeds it is impossible to find a convenient 'clear' dog, but at least you breed from a basis of knowledge and would not put a badly affected dog to a bitch showing the same affliction to an excess degree.

In breeding for a particular colour, you will need to be aware of the dominant colour in that breed; that is, the colour most likely to overcome all the others. In Labrador retrievers it was maintained that two yellow animals could not produce a black, but the dog is capable of great variation and mutations do occur, altering all the predictions of colour and marking which would have seemed to be likely. Many breeds carry a latent gene for some undesirable trait, such as a long coat in a smooth breed, or an unacceptable colour. In breeding from your pet bitch, good health and temperament should be the first virtues you are seeking to perpetuate. If your bitch has faults of temperament, it may be inbred, or the result of some trauma to the bitch while she was pregnant, or to something that has happened to the pup herself. Whatever the reason, seek perfect temperament in the stud dog, because you will be selling to pet owners who above all want a charming dog to live with.

When you have decided to breed from your bitch, you should ask for advice from her breeders. They have special interest in producing good stock in their line to enhance their reputation. If you use a friend's pet at stud, remember that you are both beginners. If you take advantage of the services of a professional stud dog on your bitch you may find that possible sales contacts are passed on to you, as well as breed knowledge. But remember this is not what you are buying with the stud fee, and the owner does not need to sell the pups for you. If sales are passed to you, it is usual to offer a 10 per cent commission, to compensate for time, trouble, and expenses.

Some stud dogs will be brought to visit the bitch, but others need the bitch brought to them; it is a matter of mutual agreement. If you are doubtful of the correct mating day, it may be best to board the bitch at the stud's premises for a few days during the

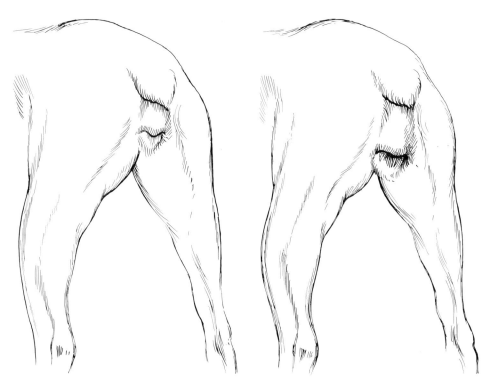

most probable period. You should have
made tentative arrangements with the stud
beforehand but you cannot make a definite
booking until the bitch shows the coloured
discharge. You should be watching for this
sign, noting the swelling of the vulva that
follows it, and testing the bitch night and
morning with a white swab. While you are
waiting it is a good idea to treat the bitch for
roundworm, whether she shows signs of
infestation or not.

On the day you see the red discharge,
book the stud by telephone at once. It is
just possible that your bitch may become
fully in season without ever showing the red
discharge – this is termed a colourless
season, but it is not usual. It is preferable to
breed from normal bitches because the condition may be hereditary. Mating is likely to
take place on any day from the tenth to four-
teenth day after showing colour in the normal
bitch. On the correct day, the vulva will have
maximum enlargement, be soft, moist, and
pink, and the discharge will have become
pale or colourless. If you pass your finger
down the bitch's spine she should stand
erect with her tail turned to one side. Do
not feed the bitch before the mating and
make sure she has had a bowel movement

and passed urine before arriving at the stud's
premises. If you are a novice at dog breeding,
allow the stud owner to organize the pro-
ceedings, and do not get nervous that your
bitch will be hurt, even if her muzzle has to
be lightly tied with a bandage to prevent
accidental injury to the male. Bitches do
sometimes cry out when the dog penetrates,
but it does not mean they are in agony. You
should try to see 'the tie', that is, the dog's
penis held fast within the bitch's vagina.
They may hold this position, turned back
to back, for twenty or thirty minutes, but it
is possible to have a satisfactory litter
without a tie because the semen is ejaculated
within the first four minutes. If there is a
tie, however, transport of the live sperm is
improved.

You must be ready to pay the mating fee
at the time of the service. You pay for the use
of the stud and not the litter. Fees vary
according to the breed and the show status
of the dog, but you should know in advance
what the fee will be. In exchange for the
stud fee you should receive a pedigree of the
dog, bearing his kennel club registration,
and a receipt for the stud fee, stating any
extra concessions or conditions made. It is
usual, but not obligatory, to offer a free stud

if the bitch does not produce a litter, if the dog is available when the bitch is in season next. The gestation period for the bitch is usually said to be sixty-three days, but she may whelp three or four days earlier, or as much as a week later, if fertilization did not take place until some time after the mating.

The bitch is still in season when you take her away after the mating, and needs increased vigilance to keep her safe. It is quite possible for a bitch to be fertilized by two dogs, or only by a second unwelcome one, after the planned mating has taken place. My advice is to forget the prospect of pregnancy for the next month. Do not increase the bitch's food, and don't keep prodding and pushing her to see if you can find any puppies, because you won't. The only thing you might do is to make extra effort to provide daily exercise, to keep her muscles in good trim. At the five weeks' stage, your bitch will probably be telling you her secret in many ways which you will notice because you know the individual animal so well. Many bitches take greater care of themselves by not jumping and running violently. They tend to lie flat on the abdomen, with the legs extended behind. The nipples begin to enlarge and show a flushed pink colouring, and usually the coat improves, giving a lovely maternal glow. You may be seeing a bulge just behind the ribs (not under the abdomen), and your bitch may have morning sickness, and an extremely variable appetite. She may also be fanciful about food, demanding one thing and refusing another. At this stage her food may be increased, and she should be fed to appetite but with the accent on protein rather than biscuit or bread. Milk and cheese added to her diet are good forms of calcium to build the puppy skeletons. If she is normally fed canned meat, or a complete diet, then the extra intake will also contain the increased vitamins she needs. If she is fed on fresh meat and biscuit, however, increase the bone flour and codliver oil in direct proportion to the amount of food. She will not need a great deal extra.

During the last week of pregnancy you should be able to see the puppies moving when the bitch is lying on her side. In any case, it is wise during the last week to have her examined by your veterinary surgeon who can then detect the foetal hearts and know that all is well. Should your bitch have a coloured discharge from the vulva during pregnancy, or seem ill, get professional help at once. During the last weeks the bitch will need to be fed several small meals a day, and it is possible that she may have to urinate during the night owing to pressure on the bladder. She must be forgiven lapses at this stage.

For a first litter, it is best not to buy any whelping equipment until you are sure you will need it, but everything should be arranged two weeks before the due date. The bitch needs a warm, secluded place, in semi-darkness, and preferably with access to the garden. It should also be a reasonably familiar place in which she will be happy. She will not do well in the hall or the kitchen where there are constant comings and goings nor in a place open to the gaze of strangers. The bitch is at her most protective when she has young puppies, and she will lie on them, or hide them, if she feels they are threatened, and in doing so, may injure them. In most homes a garden room, a second bathroom, or a spare bedroom are the best choices for whelping quarters. It is useful to have somewhere which has running water available, which is easy to clean, draughtproof, and with room for an attendant to sleep close by. Heating must raise the temperature to 75 °F (24 °C) but there must be ventilation, and curtains or blinds so that the room is like the dark, warm tunnel which the bitch would choose herself. Watch her when she goes into the garden during the last week, because she may try to dig a place for herself. Exercise is very important while the bitch is pregnant. This is the one time when I concentrate on controlled lead exercise, without other dogs present that may bump the pregnant bitch.

The whelping box for a big dog should fit her length when she lies on her side at full stretch. A small dog may be accommodated in her own wooden box, or basket, with the soft bedding removed and replaced by newspaper. Newspaper is an essential to whelping and you will need all you can get. We prefer unsold copies from newsagents rather than an assortment collected from friends and neighbours that may be contaminated in some way. Cloth or sacking should not be used for a whelping bed, because the pups may smother in it, but newspaper shreds up well and is easily disposable. As you approach whelping time, the bitch should

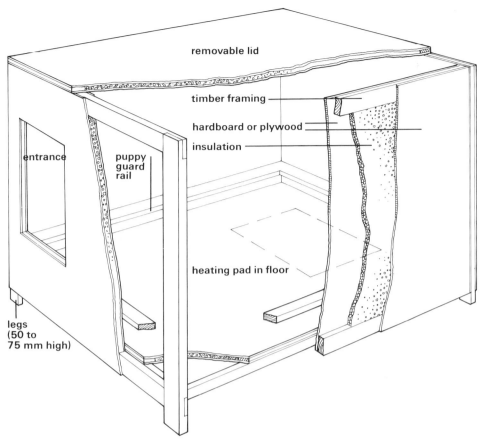

Insulated whelping box designed to conserve body heat of the bitch. Insulation material must be inert and non-fibrous.

removable lid

timber framing

hardboard or plywood

insulation

entrance

puppy guard rail

heating pad in floor

legs (50 to 75 mm high)

not be left alone for long, and must not be left in furnished rooms where she may start to make a nest in upholstered furniture.

Make sure that your veterinary surgeon can be contacted at any time at night or during the weekend if necessary. Litters may take as long as twenty-four hours to be born, and the veterinary surgeon cannot be in attendance all the time, but you will want help if your bitch is in trouble. If you have a breed in which it is customary to dock tails, you should find out if the veterinary practice will be willing to do this for you.

The first sign of imminent whelping is usually a complete refusal of food, for twenty-four hours before whelping. This is useful because the bitch enters into the ordeal without a full intestine. You will notice a discharge from the vulva, thin at first, then becoming more profuse. Milk may have been let down into the mammary glands, or may only come after the pups are born. Your bitch will be restless at this stage, shivering, panting very deeply, and rising periodically to shred up her bed. Bitches have very firm ideas about where

they would like to have their pups, and may hold up if their wishes are not gratified. You may decide to let her have the first puppy in the place of her choice, and then move her and the first-born to the whelping room where she is likely to settle. Make sure that the room is really warm, according to the heat tolerance of your particular breed. Another smaller box with a hot water bottle is useful should the bitch not want her puppies with her until whelping is finished. You will need plenty of old towelling which you can throw away afterwards because it will stain when you are drying the pups. You should also have gauze in small pieces to swab the puppies' mouths, tissues, a plastic sack for wet paper, and a lidded bucket of water to take placentas (afterbirth) if they cannot go straight down the WC.

You will need a glucose drink for the bitch, possibly some brandy for both owner and bitch, and a feeding bottle with appropriately sized teats, and some specially formulated milk powder for puppies in case they are not able to suck or the bitch does not let down milk. There are excellent chemically formulated milks on the market; remember that human baby milk does not contain the correct nutrients. Long-haired bitches should have their coats trimmed around the nipples and hindquarters, and all will benefit from being wiped with a mild germicidal solution. Have a basin of hot water, a nailbrush, and a good soap or surgical scrub available in case you or the veterinary surgeon need to make an internal investigation, and provide an examination table in a good light.

WHELPING

Try to notice the time of the first major bearing down pain, because if there is a hold-up the veterinary surgeon will want to know. Some bitches squeal a little at the first pains, others are very stoical. This is a time to provide the utmost calm for the bitch. You should certainly not allow an interested audience to be present, and you must not show any signs of anxiety. Most pet bitches like to have someone with them, some will need your active attention, to the extent of holding her paw, while with others you will sense that by hovering around the box you are preventing her concentrating on her job. An ideal solution is to be in the room with some other occupation which you can cease when necessary. The first stage of labour when the passages are dilating causes the bitch minimal discomfort, but she is apprehensive and cannot settle. Some will fret for long periods, others will pass the first puppy before you, or she, are aware of it. If you are an inexperienced dog breeder you must contact the vet if more than twenty-four hours have elapsed after the expected whelping time with no result.

From the first major labour pain, the vulva, vagina, and cervix should be wide open, and the puppy will be making its

Beagle bitch, Champion Crestamere Orchid. A confident dam not disturbed by the camera at her whelping. 1 Water bag emerging from the vulva.

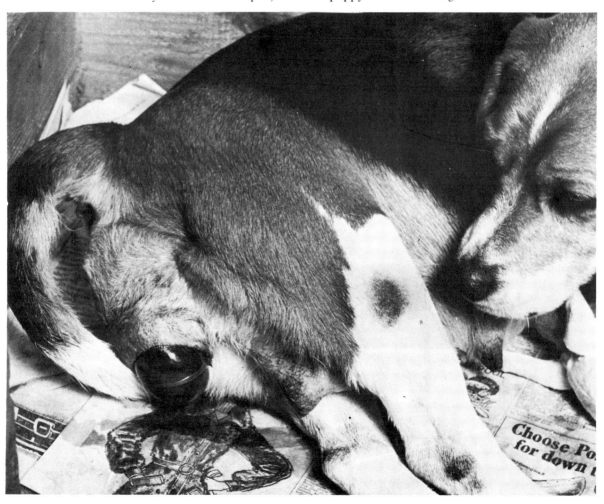

descent. Each puppy will be in its double layered water bag, followed quickly by its own placenta. The flexible bag of amniotic fluid in which the pup has grown makes its way along by hydraulic pressure, over the edge of the pelvic bone, down through the vagina and out into the world. The first sign you will see will be a black balloon containing the puppy, unless you have already seen a burst of greenish black fluid, which will mean that the bag has burst, when you may see a recognizable puppy head, or perhaps hind feet and tail. A hind presentation is so common as not to cause distress except with breeds which have very wide shoulders. The puppy does not always descend quickly, and the bitch may need to make several strains and bearing-down movements, before the pup is expelled. Once a puppy is in view, it must be removed quickly, or it will die. Obviously, if there is an obstruction at this stage you do not have time to get veterinary help, and if the pup is within your grasp, scrub your hands, leaving them wet and soapy, take hold of the pup with a piece of clean towelling and pull forwards very gently, a fraction at a time, with the bitch's contractions. Directly the puppy is out, break the bag with your fingernail, free the puppy, cleaning it at mouth and nostrils so that it does not take fluid and debris into the lungs. You may hold the puppy up by the back feet to do this. The bitch may be anxious to lick the pup and help you, or she may be tired and bewildered leaving you to cope. It does not matter if the umbilical cord is still attached, or even that the placenta has not appeared. Ensure that the pup is breathing and tidy up later. The placenta may arrive soon, and you may then sever the umbilical cord; it is safest to do this with your finger nails, or failing that, sterilized scissors. Make the cut a long way from the puppy, leaving an end of not less

2 Puppy is still encased in membranes, almost delivered. The bitch is ready to tear open the bag and clean her puppy.

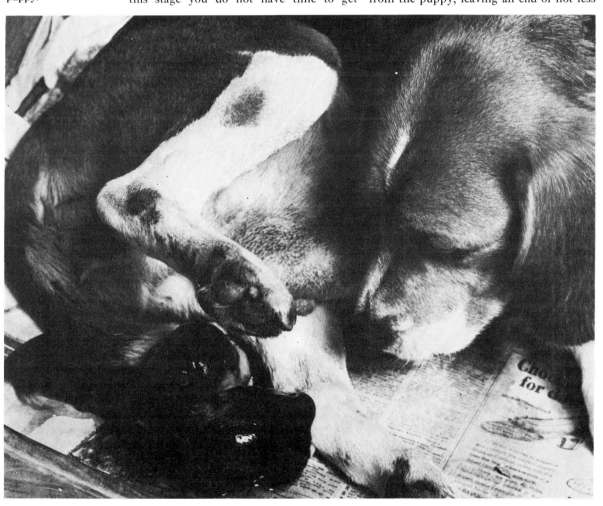

than 1·5 inches (3·75 centimetres), which will drop off in time. There is no need to tie or seal the cord in any way. It may be that your bitch will have forestalled you by biting off the cord, and eating the placenta. I let my bitches have some placentas, but try to remove at least half, because eating too many causes a looseness of the bowels which can be a nuisance.

As the bitch's abdomen decreases in size and she begins to understand what is happening, she will be quicker to get to the pups as they are born and will probably do all the work herself, including eating the placenta before you are aware of it. The veterinary surgeon is sure to ask you if you can account for all placentas, because a retained one is a danger. Don't worry if you

can't, I have never been able to. In a healthy bitch a retained placenta may be passed without trouble some two days after whelping, and if one is causing poisoning, you should notice it and arrange for her to have treatment which will expel it fast.

You should help the bitch to dry the puppies, because the sooner they are warm and dry the better. If she is inclined to be too rough with the pups they should be removed until she is more relaxed. It is natural and purposeful that a bitch shall lick her puppies quite vigorously to stimulate breathing and have them pass their first excreta, which she will clear up. Strong puppies will then find their way to a teat and begin suckling. This aids the let down of milk if none is yet present. The bitch may

3 New-born puppy
with umbilical cord
severed.

take an hour or more to rest before beginning to strain for another puppy, and you need to be watching the time carefully, to be ready to ask for help if the hold up is too long. A delay of two hours is becoming serious, but your breed advisor can help you here, because some are notoriously slow whelpers. If you are reluctant to contact your veterinary surgeon, an experienced breeder can be a great help. If there is a serious delay during whelping, or if the bitch has not enough hormonal stimulus to begin expelling at all, the vet may inject your bitch to induce uterine contractions, or may remove the puppies with forceps. In the case of absolute obstruction the bitch may have to go to the surgery for delivery by caesarian section. The outlook for dam and pups is now very good, and you should not worry too much although, of course, a normal delivery is preferable. The important thing is not to delay getting help, if you think you need it, at any stage of whelping. If the veterinary surgeon asks you to drive the bitch to the surgery, this does not indicate lack of concern because the movement of your car will often stimulate a whelping and, of course, the surgery is a more suitable place for examination and manipulation if necessary. Keep the bitch warm on the journey, however, and have someone to steady her in the car. Many bitches like a drink between puppies, and if there is a delay, a visit to the garden may often get things moving, and a puppy may emerge when she squats to urinate; so watch her carefully, especially at night.

It is useful to keep a note of the times the pups were born and note any identifying markings; some breeders like to weigh each pup at birth. If all is going well, your job will be to change the newspapers under the bitch regularly and to dry the puppies every time they become soiled by the water bags of new arrivals. The production of milk for pups demands that the bitch takes a lot of fluid, and you should provide water as well as milk drinks. All will have to be offered to her in her bed, because she will not leave it. My bitches are all fed and watered in their whelping beds for about two weeks after the birth because most will not willingly leave, even if they are hungry and thirsty. The animal which is especially devoted to you will sometimes indicate that she wants you to take her pups wherever you are, and in

this case you must oblige, and provide a mobile whelping box for a dam with divided loyalties. The bitch that wants nothing to do with her pups and curls into a tight ball refusing to let them feed is surely indicating that something is physically wrong. In the meantime, you must bottle-feed the pups at two-hourly intervals day and night according to the manufacturer's instructions for the milk. It is necessary to have the bottle and the milk powder in stock, because if you do need it, you want it immediately available.

The normal, healthy bitch should lie stretched out on her side, with all the pups feeding when she has finished her whelping. For the first few days she will have to be firmly persuaded to go into the garden to evacuate. While you are outside with her insisting that she remains as long as necessary, another person can clean up her box. Some degree of diarrhoea is to be expected because of all the body fluids which have been ingested. In every case, however easy the whelping, you should have the vet check the pups and the bitch the next day, even if you find the pups have arrived unexpectedly in the night. The bitch may have a slightly raised temperature for a few days after whelping. For the first two days she should be fed on egg custards, milk puddings, and milky drinks. Then she progresses to fish and white meat if she is doing well. After that she will have a voracious appetite, depending on the size of her litter. She can then revert to her normal food, but as much as 100 per cent more than usual, with meals served at frequent intervals. She will otherwise draw on her own resources and end her lactation period a disgrace to you, at the very time when you are selling the puppies and want her to look attractive. Plenty of water and milk must be available. This is the expensive time in dog breeding, but the bitch needs plenty of food so that she can provide nutrition for her puppies. All your efforts will have been wasted if you are not generous at this time.

The bitch will have some discharge from the vulva for some weeks after whelping. If the discharge is dark, greenish, or foul smelling, and the bitch is not eating, and her temperature at the rectum is above 102 °F (39 °C) then you need veterinary help. Never be slow in contacting the vet at this time because infections develop so fast in little puppies and in the open uterus of

Above **Border collie working in an obedience competition.**
Left **The ultimate accolade in the beauty show: Supreme Best in Show at Cruft's, Miss Violet Drummond-Dick's bull terrier Abraxas Audacity.**
Right **A Labrador awaiting its turn at a field trial.**

the bitch. Keep a watch on the mammary glands, to see that none is becoming hard, red, and inflamed, indicating that there is a mastitis there. While awaiting veterinary help you may poultice the gland with hot flannels.

Puppies that cry constantly, that move away from the bitch and lie passively in a corner are an indication that something is wrong. Litters are usually quite large and owners should resolve themselves to the fact that pups may be born with congenital defects, or may be injured at birth, and it is useless and also unethical to struggle to keep them alive. While you may feel a sense of pride in rearing an undersized pup by hand it is more than likely that the animal will have only a short life and may die at one or two years old from a defect of the heart, brain, or skeleton. It is as well to be aware, however, that in many breeds the new pups do not look like the adults, or even the six week puppy you bought; do not discard a pup because you think the colour is wrong before asking an experienced breeder's advice.

During the first three weeks of the puppies' lives they need seclusion and very restricted visiting. If the bitch is worried about the safety of her pups, she may try to hide them and injure them in doing so. Some bitches become so agitated about their pups that they lick them too vigorously, taking the skin off their abdomens. This, I think, gives rise to the rumour that bitches may eat their pups, because I have never known this to happen. Some of the heavy breed bitches will lay on their pups and squash one inadvertantly. If you are nearby you can rescue the screaming pup. Some whelping boxes are provided with rails to hold the bitch away from the box sides,

4 Litter safely delivered, dry, and feeding, about four hours old.

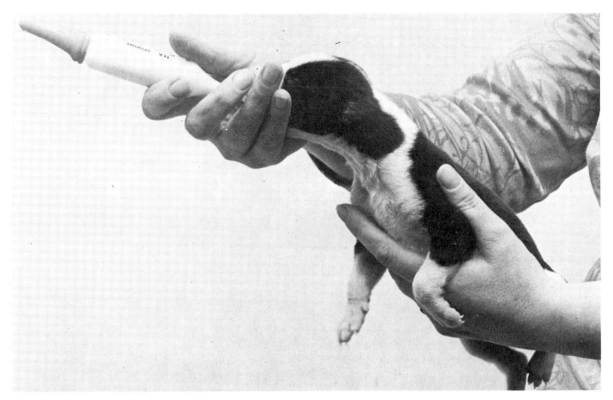

5 Correct position for supplementary bottle feeding.

allowing a creep for the puppies, but more recently we have abandoned this idea in favour of a piece of heated floor in the box on which the pups tend to congregate when not feeding. You will observe changes in the pups daily, such as the eyes beginning to open at ten to fourteen days, the ears developing, and hearing becoming apparent. I do not take lactating bitches for exercise; the garden is enough for them and gives less risk of bringing infection in to the pups. Puppy nails should be trimmed once weekly and navels inspected regularly to ensure that no infection is present.

When the pups are twenty-one days old they should be just about getting to their feet, and this is the time to allow visitors to come and play gently and handle them. Behavioural studies have shown that the twenty-first day of life is the crucial one for the newborn dog to make attachments to humans. Puppies which are not handled and integrated with people from the twenty-first day until the forty-second day will always be more wild and unresponsive, and never make such agreeable pets. They should now be moved to larger quarters, where they can learn to move about, and where the bitch is more free to leave them if she

wishes. She should be provided with a bed out of reach of the pups. The pups will need warmth at night, and ideally they should be in the house where they can see and hear all the activities of humans to condition them for a pet life to come. In good weather a moveable playpen on the lawn is particularly good for puppies, but remember to provide some shade, and shelter from winds. Young puppies do not tolerate bright light and may huddle away with heads hidden.

At twenty-one days, or a little later in some breeds, the pups should begin to be weaned. They can be offered egg custard, cereal and milk, or one of the complete diets in a flat baking tin. The first few meals are always wasted, the pups just paddling through them and licking the food off each other, but this messy process is necessary to accustom them to the new way of taking nourishment. You may despair that they will ever learn, but in the end they do, one after the other. If the dam is willing to leave them, it helps to take her away for an hour before you feed the pups. They should begin with one dish a day, and then two, and as they begin to eat strongly they can be fed four times a day, with the dam coming and

The boxer is a modern creation bred from a German Bullenbeisser crossed with an English bull-dog, creating a dog with controlled guard instincts and equable disposition in the home.

The bulldog is renowned for its tenacity and originally took part in bull baiting which was a popular sport.

Above The mastiff is thought to have been brought to England with the Romans. The breed has been adopted by man for many purposes employing the natural attributes of strength and guarding ability in a variety of ways.

Right The bull mastiff was traditionally the gamekeeper's night dog.

going at will. She should be in the room with them at night, but free to move away if she wants. She must be provided with a separate bed that the puppies cannot reach. Continue to trim the pups' toe nails every week, and examine each dog daily.

At this stage, more than any other, you must watch your bitch closely for signs of lactation tetany, an imbalance of calcium which may be the result of a drain on her resources through milk production. It even affects bitches that have had the benefit of perfect vitamin and calcium balance and is partly hereditary. The early signs, apparent to the watchful owner may be summed up as 'doing things she would not normally do'. In my bitches the signs have varied from suddenly tearing up her bed, to hiding, or attempting to run up the wall. Another sign is chewing plaster from the walls, or you may find the bitch in a state of collapse. Veterinary help is needed fast, day or night. This is a condition where you must not hesitate to trouble the vet; an immediate injection can reverse the state like magic, neglect could bring almost certain death.

When the puppies begin to eat for themselves, the bitch will cease to clean up the excreta, although she will still clean the pups. Putting down fresh paper every time it is soiled is a time-consuming job but nothing looks worse than dirty puppies. The colour and texture of the excreta tells a lot about the condition of the puppies. You should try to ensure that they pass a formed motion, which will be yellow on cereal and milk feeding, and darker if you have begun to give scraped or minced meat balanced with cereal.

The puppies will need their first worming for round worm when they are between twenty-one and twenty-eight days old. Separate the bitch from them for some hours, because you do not want her to ingest the worms. The dose should be prescribed by your vet and not bought over the counter. Give the prescribed dose individually to each pup; with a big litter it is useful to worm each sex or colour on a different day, so that you know each pup has reacted. All puppies have worms, but the object is to rid the dogs of them as quickly as possible. The worms should begin to emerge after the next meal. You will see the string-like worms with the excreta, and the process continues for about eighteen hours.

You should always be ready to pick up and burn the worms or put them down the WC as they are voided. Scrupulous hand cleanliness is necessary, particularly before you prepare any food, and children are best kept away. The process is repeated in fourteen days, but there should be fewer worms this time. I always worm the bitch at this time too. Do not evade the worming session by thinking that *your* pups do not have any. Find out by treating them.

Little pups play wildly and noisily, but they sleep a lot too, and must be allowed long periods of undisturbed rest between visiting. Young children should be asked to sit on the floor when handling pups, because they are so easily dropped.

You should now begin the task of making out the pedigrees for the pups, putting the sire's on the top half of the form, and the dam's at the bottom. Send to the kennel club for the appropriate forms if you wish to register them before sale, or if you wish to register a prefix to be exclusively your own. You should try to register puppies when they are about five weeks old. If you mean to keep one, now is the time to decide, so that it will not be offered for choice by anyone else. It is silly to have gone to all this trouble and then to retain the one that was slow to sell. Expect to spend the selling price of one puppy on advertising in national evening papers, Sunday editions, and the local papers, as well as the dog weeklies and specialist papers for gundogs or hounds. There is also a very worthwhile Breeders' Agency which you may join on recommendation, which circularizes the names of people inquiring for a puppy, taking a very small commission for the trouble. You may put notices in pet shops, and don't forget to remind your vet that you have a nice litter. A telephone number is essential because most preliminary inquiries are made that way.

Purchasers have the right to expect that you will provide the pup's pedigree, and a diet sheet, showing how it is being fed, and possibly some hints for future management. Puppies sold uninoculated should have a note made on the pedigree of the date when the dam had her last booster course, for the guidance of the new veterinary surgeon. It is also helpful to give the address of suppliers for food, breed clubs and local canine societies, and training clubs. A note of books that

The first taste of solid food.

you have found helpful would also be a generous gesture. The time for selling puppies is usually quoted as at eight weeks old, but the latest information from the dog psychologists tells us that this age approximates to the well-known eight-month old 'fear period' in human children. We are advised that upsets and new experiences are best avoided between the eighth and ninth weeks. Strong puppies of the larger breeds may go to experienced owners, without small children, at six weeks, with a great deal of information about their care. The puppies will become very closely identified with their owners. Small breed puppies, or those destined for busy or noisy households are best retained by the breeder until nine weeks of age. We like our owners to collect early on a Saturday morning, so that they may have all the weekend with the pup, and we like two people to come to collect, so that the first car ride is undertaken in someone's arms. It is almost inevitable that carefully

as you have picked your purchasers, someone's life style will change, or they will find they don't like dogs after all. While not offering an easy way to get rid of the pup the first time it offends them, I try to indicate that I will always be glad to see it as it grows, and to advise if needed. I hope that if there is to be a parting, I would be the first to know.

All dogs give problems as they grow up, and sometimes a little advice at the crucial time may enable owners to retain a dog that they are beginning to think is impossible. If they are determined to part with the animal, it is much better that it comes back to the breeder rather than going to a public rescue society. You probably will not want to take a delinquent dog, house it for a while, retrain and get it another home, but this is ultimately the breeder's responsibility, and part of the pleasure and the pain to be taken into account when you consider breeding from your bitch.

Left The Boston terrier is a native of America, probably a cross between a bull-dog and bull terrier.

Below A French bulldog is characterized by erect ears and, once a fighting dog, still shows determination and tenacity.

Right The bulldog crossed with terrier breeds resulted in a more agile dog with fighting instincts.

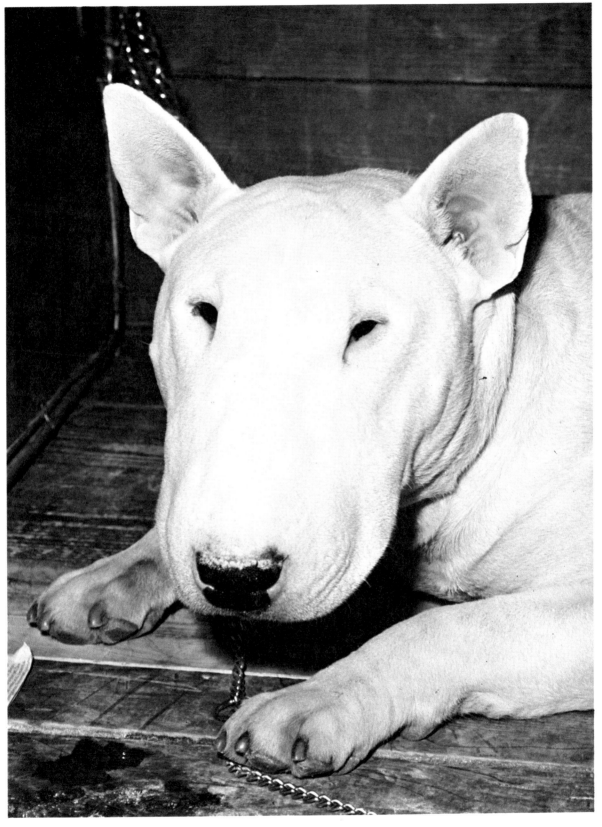

Ill health

INTRODUCTION

Most dogs enjoy remarkably healthy lives but it would be unrealistic to suggest that any individual is likely to come to the end of its days without ever requiring attention for some illness or injury. Indeed, before making the final decision to acquire a canine pet it is imperative that prospective owners face the problem posed by nursing a sick animal if they have to be away from home for much of the day.

Ill health really comprises a departure from normal health, and it is vital for owners to be able to recognize what is usual for each particular dog. You must learn the dog's normal eating pattern – whether it has a voracious appetite or an intermittent one; you must know what is its normal excretory function of bowels and bladder – some dogs will defecate (pass a motion) once daily, some twice daily and a few will miss a day or days without any cause for alarm; dogs vary greatly in their water intake – young puppies seldom drink water but adults drink differing amounts; some dogs occasionally vomit a little yellow fluid or froth (bile) without there being any cause for alarm.

So the watchword is close daily observation of all normal bodily functions and behaviour; this can be done very easily, almost subconsciously, if you cultivate the habit of noticing. If you notice any change then you should watch even more closely; for example, a dog may strain a lot when defecating due to constipation or diarrhoea – diametrically opposite conditions yet a similar symptom.

On the other hand, you should not be too fussy and worry unnecessarily; some people identify so closely with their pets that they become almost neurotic – this is no good to man nor beast.

LINKING UP WITH A VETERINARY PRACTICE

Even if the services of a veterinary surgeon are not required to treat illness or injury all responsible owners will wish to take advantage of prophylactic (disease prevention) measures. Hence, some call on veterinary service is inevitable.

Despite modernization many veterinary practices retain a degree of the family doctor approach, and most veterinary surgeons appreciate the opportunity of seeing a patient through most of its life. You should choose a suitable practice and contact the veterinary surgeon soon after buying a dog. Then try to remain a regular client (all other things being equal, of course) rather than to go to whatever practice happens to come to mind or whose surgery hours suit at the particular time. A careful and comprehensive clinical record can be kept of regular patients – impossible with the casual caller – and this is a tremendous advantage to all.

HOW TO USE YOUR VETERINARY SURGEON

Having selected the practice to which you hope to go, telephone the receptionist to find out how that practice is organized; for example, are there consulting hours, or is it an appointment system? do they do house calls (less and less practices are doing so under modern conditions)? will you be able to see the same veterinary surgeon on most occasions or do you have to accept whoever is on duty when you call? Once you know the routine you can decide if it suits your requirements and, having decided, there is the basis for a rewarding relationship.

In addition, find out when it is possible to speak personally with a veterinary surgeon – interrupting a consultation or leaving an operation to speak on the telephone cannot be done. You must also ask how early you should 'phone for an appointment or visit. Many people fail to realize the difference between medical and veterinary practice. The veterinary surgeon not only acts as a physician but is usually a skilled surgeon, performing several operations daily. He or she is also dental surgeon, ophthalmologist, obstetrician, and casualty officer; quite a full daily life by any standard.

Veterinary surgeons are usually extremely busy and will not thank you for repeated panic calls for trivialities. Equally, they realize that the owner often cannot distinguish between the major and the minor and your worries will receive sympathetic hearing. On the other hand, undue delay in seeking veterinary advice may jeopardize a dog's chances of recovery and this, too, is disliked by the veterinary surgeon who detests being handicapped from the start in saving life or restoring to health. The owner who manages to achieve just the right balance is much prized!

HISTORY OF THE CASE

Animals cannot describe their own symptoms, and you must provide the veterinary surgeon with a good history based on sound observation; these are objective as opposed to subjective signs. Always answer questions factually, and do not attempt to guess the reasons for asking, perhaps giving the answer you think is wanted; you will often be wrong anyway and it is facts that matter.

The veterinary surgeon will probably want to know:

age of patient;

sex – *not* always self-evident in a long-coated breed – and will include whether neutered or not;

how long you have owned the dog, and from where it came if acquired recently, for example, private breeder, pet shop, dealing kennels, dogs' home or perhaps a purely private home;

if the dog was adult when you bought it what was the reason for sale?

immune status, that is, what vaccinations has the dog had and when? (it is most helpful if certificates of vaccination can be produced);

previous health history;

duration of present illness;

state of appetite;

change in behaviour, for example, quieter than usual;

vomiting, diarrhoea, consistency and colour of faeces (motion);

any sign of cough and if so its character;

abnormal posture when standing, sitting, or lying;

increase or decrease in water intake;

urination pattern, for example, does the male dog still lift his leg?

change in body weight – often deceptive because an enlarged abdomen may give the impression of fatness yet the dog is really losing weight;

exercise tolerance – can he go as far as usual without getting tired?

All these and many more questions may be asked and sometimes a particular aspect will be followed up in great detail.

A good, clear history is extremely valuable.

DIFFERENTIAL DIAGNOSIS

I shall often suggest times when it would be wise or even essential to take your dog to the veterinary surgeon. This is not an advertisement for veterinary practice. It is in the interests of both dog and owner because the key to satisfactory treatment is differential diagnosis, that is, the attempt to arrive at a precise diagnosis of the condition from which the dog is suffering. This is not always possible at the first visit nor always as easy as it might seem. Often a clinical sign (symptom) such as increased water intake, is common to a number of diseases, some serious and some trivial. It is only by a careful consideration of all the facts, possibly assisted by various specialized examinations in addition to the routine clinical examination, that diseases can be differentiated and an accurate diagnosis be arrived at.

Diagnosis is rather like a detective problem, and the veterinary surgeon is trained to assess the relative significance of the various symptoms and findings – the clues – and eventually arrive at the correct solution. This can be quick and easy, all done at the first consultation, or it may take quite some time to sort out satisfactorily. This may puzzle and worry the anxious owner, yet a soundly based diagnosis is far better for the patient than an inspired 'guess' made under pressure from the owner.

EXAMINATION OF A NEW PURCHASE

If you are not experienced with dogs you would be wise to have the new arrival examined by a veterinary surgeon within the first twenty-four hours. Reputable breeders

Left **Irish setter pups need work and games devised to keep them exercised and interested to develop their many talents.**

Right **This Yorkshire terrier pup has yet to grow the long, silky coat characteristic of the adult.**

will not usually object if you suggest that the sale is confirmed after an examination.

Not only will the veterinary surgeon look for evidence of infectious disease, malnutrition, and infestation with parasites but will also look for any evidence of congenital abnormalities, that is, problems that the puppy was born with. The veterinary surgeon sees many breeds of dog in the day's work, and knows which breeds are especially liable to some of these congenital conditions, such as hernias (ruptures), dislocating patella (kneecap), in-turned eyelids (entropion), and so on. It is much better to know from the beginning whether the new purchase is sound and well nourished, or if something wrong is found to know what is its significance and the future outlook. To face problems at an early stage is far easier than after a few weeks, or even days, by which time the new owner will have formed a close attachment to the pup.

PROPHYLAXIS – PREVENTION OF DISEASE

Many infectious diseases, whether due to viruses (germs which can pass through an ultra-microscopic filter) or bacteria (which do not pass through) can be prevented by vaccination.

Immunity is a highly complex subject but a very brief description may be helpful. When an infective agent invades the animal body certain immune responses are triggered off, resulting in the formation of antibodies which appear in the blood or tissue cells about ten to twenty-one days after infection enters. These antibodies counteract the invading germs with varying success; if they succeed completely the disease is overcome and the animal recovers, but if they are partially successful the multiplication of organisms is slowed down and as a rule eventual recovery takes place; if they fail and the disease is a severe one the animal dies.

The purpose of vaccination is to introduce into an animal the particular disease organism in such a form that it will stimulate an immune response specific to that disease without causing any illness or at most a very mild infection. This is active immunization.

A young puppy inherits some passive immunity from its dam, either from the maternal blood while it is still in the uterus (womb) or from the colostrum – the special first milk produced by the bitch for twelve to twenty-four hours after whelping. The degree of passive immunity that a puppy receives will depend on the immune status of the dam before and at whelping and this in turn depends on whether she has had certain infections or whether she is fully vaccinated. This variable degree of passive immunity creates problems in deciding at what age puppies are best vaccinated.

Passive immunity can also be provided by injecting hyperimmune serum into the sick animal, always provided such a serum is available; some sera are extremely effective but the number of really effective ones available for dogs is limited.

Vaccines vary in type and their manufacture and subsequent testing for efficacy and safety is a highly complex and costly procedure. Virus vaccines may be living but attenuated, that is, the virus is produced in such a way that it is not able to cause infection but will provoke an immune response. They may also be killed vaccines which obviously cannot cause disease but provoke some degree of immunity that is rather less effective and long lasting than the living vaccine, but can still be perfectly satisfactory when used correctly.

Four diseases of dogs are normally controlled by vaccination in Britain. The diseases are: canine distemper, due to a virus; canine virus hepatitis (Rubarth's disease); leptospirosis in two forms. Vaccination against rabies is not permitted in Britain except under certain specialized conditions such as in quarantine kennels, and can only be carried out by veterinary personnel of the Ministry of Fisheries and Food.

CANINE DISTEMPER

Very effective vaccination is available and provided the conditions laid down by the veterinary surgeon as regards age, isolation, and so on are adhered to, more than 90 per cent of puppies can be protected. For some reason not understood about 3 per cent of dogs do not respond to vaccination.

CANINE VIRUS HEPATITIS

Both dead and live vaccines are available and immunization with either is effective.

LEPTOSPIROSIS

Leptospires are bacteria in the form of

microscopic corkscrews and there are many different strains. The two important bacteria for which vaccination is available are:

Leptospira canicola, which causes damage to the kidneys, and even if the primary disease is mild the long-term effects can be serious and will often shorten a dog's life; *L. icterohaemorrhagiae*, which causes a much more severe and often fatal disease with jaundice and kidney lesions.

Protection is afforded by killed bacterial vaccines which give effective but relatively short-lived immunity. Hence, annual booster doses are essential.

The virus vaccines give a more durable immunity but if the dog does not bolster its immunity by contact with naturally occurring disease, it will eventually wane. Usually, the dog should have boosters at an interval which will be recommended by the veterinary surgeon whose knowledge of the canine disease pattern in the particular locality will enable him or her to forecast how often repeat vaccinations are needed.

It is because of the variability of local conditions that veterinary surgeons in different areas may differ from one another both in the recommended age for initial vaccination and in how often boosters are to be administered – it is not just a personal whim.

The standard of vaccination available for dogs is very high indeed and if you meticulously follow the advice of the veterinary surgeon before and after vaccination you can be fairly confident that your pet is well protected against the major infections common in the dog.

THE YOUNG PUPPY

To be able to detect departures from normal health it is essential to have a sound knowledge of the normal behaviour pattern in this age group.

For the first few weeks after weaning the puppy sleeps for a large proportion of its time and it must be allowed to do so. The pattern is sleep, on waking the pup urinates, and it then seeks food. After this it will have a period of play during which it will again pass urine and probably a motion as well. Finally, it will settle to sleep again. As each week passes the duration of play periods increases and sleep decreases until by ten to twelve weeks of age the pup is awake most of the day. Once a routine is established a healthy puppy seldom cries other than to attract attention when wanting to go out, or come out of a particular place, or to obtain the owner's attention.

UNDUE CRYING
The newly acquired pup will cry at first when left alone, having lost contact with its dam and litter mates, but this is not abnormal. Excessive crying once the pup is acclimatized to its new surroundings, however, may indicate discomfort and if accompanied by loss of appetite, diarrhoea, or a 'pot belly' may be due to some digestive upset and veterinary advice should be sought. It will rarely be serious but if anything causes irregular bowel contraction a telescoping of segments of bowel can very occasionally occur (intussusception) and this requires prompt attention.

POOR APPETITE
Most young pups have a healthy appetite but breeds vary considerably in this respect and while some will gorge themselves if given the chance others only eat to satisfaction. The lack of competition from litter mates may initially cause a pup to show less interest in food but this should right itself in a few days.

Missing an occasional meal is not a cause for alarm but failure to take several meals in succession or a sudden loss of appetite in a previously good eater should not be ignored. The possible reasons for this are very numerous, and it is important to seek professional advice to make the necessary differential diagnosis.

DIARRHOEA
It is quite common for the new puppy to develop diarrhoea. Defecation becomes more frequent and the motion more fluid than usual. Change of diet and surroundings may easily cause a transient diarrhoea but this should quickly settle. If diarrhoea persists the cause again may be one of many. A few are listed below.

Incorrect feeding It is surprising how often owners give very young puppies diets designed for adult dogs in a way they would never do with a human infant. A revision of the diet may put things right.

Vitamin deficiency An occasional cause

of diarrhoea but vitamin therapy should not be tried without professional advice because just as much harm can result from too high a vitamin intake or an incorrect balance between vitamins as from a deficiency.

Enteritis (inflammation of the bowel) This can be due to infection or mechanical causes. Enteritis can occur in virus infections or it can be due to bacteria. Puppies which have been obtained from pet shops or dealing kennels where many litters from different sources mix together may acquire a bacterial infection as a result of picking up a germ which is a normal inhabitant in the gut in one litter but can cause problems in another. Mechanical causes include the eating of foreign substances, usually in play, such as wood shavings used for bedding, grit, small stones, bits of chewed wood, and so on. Puppies should be supplied with toys of a type which cannot give rise to these problems.

Change in behaviour, that is, less playful If a pup suddenly becomes dull and unresponsive and is not playful after a normal rest period you should seek advice because apathetic behaviour is a sign common to many illnesses.

'Pot belly' This is the term given to an animal which is often in poor bodily condition but which has a large abdomen. A puppy should be evenly plump all over and the abdomen should not be particularly noticeable. Faulty nutrition may be the cause as may a heavy infestation with worms.

Worms There are basically two types of intestinal worms which infest dogs, these are, round worms and tapeworms. Tapeworms are not often important in young puppies.

Round worms are important in young puppies and there are two main species seen, the more important being *Toxocara canis*. This worm is important because it has an unusual life cycle and puppies become infested from the dam before birth while they are still in the womb. The worms mature quickly and can, if numerous, cause ill-health in puppies as young as three or four weeks; they may cause symptoms in puppies up to eight or nine weeks but seldom cause much trouble in older animals. There is a very slight risk of humans, particularly young children, being invaded by *Toxocara canis*. Regular routine dosing of all dogs, especially puppies between two to three

Round worms (ascarids) are seen expelled with faeces. These worms are approximately 2 mm in diameter and 50 to 150 mm long.

weeks and one year of age, is recommended; annual dosing of adult dogs is also wise. Owners can also help by a responsible attitude to the removal and safe disposal of dog faeces from any place accessible to the public and/or other dogs.

Treatment for worms is best done with veterinary advice to ensure that the most effective drugs are used on a properly estimated dosage based on each dog's body weight.

Biting or licking under the tail or rubbing the bottom on the floor are not signs of worms as is usually believed. As a rule, you can see a worm or worms in the motion as a creamy white, slightly coiled worm which tapers at both ends. Alternatively, if worms are suspected the veterinary surgeon can very easily make a diagnosis by examining a specimen of faeces under the microscope to look for worm eggs.

Scratching Most dogs scratch occasionally, and puppies are no exception, but excessive, frequent scratching is a sign of trouble. The commonest causes of scratching in pups are various external parasites. Some, such as fleas and lice, are visible to the naked eye while others, such as the mange mites, can only be seen under the microscope. Fleas are seen as brownish insects, moving in the depth of the coat, often over the lower part of the back, near the base of the tail. Lice do not move and are seen as bluish-grey or light brown parasites attached to the skin; the ear flaps are a common site especially in dogs with well-feathered ears such as spaniels. The mange mites require specialized diagnostic methods to detect. Because the drugs used to disinfest animals are required to kill the parasites they are obviously to some extent toxic, and while they are safe if used correctly on adult dogs their use on young puppies requires the greatest care. It is best done under veterinary supervision both as to selection of the agent and method of application. The frequency of application will depend on the life cycle of the parasite concerned so that once again a careful diagnosis is important.

THE GROWING PUP

Puppies in the nest grow very fast from three to six weeks of age, and once the check of weaning is passed the growing pup, say from eight to fourteen weeks of age, continues to grow and gain weight very fast, thereafter slowing down to some extent. An example would be of a breed which will reach adult weight of about 60 pounds (27 kilograms) such pups will gain 1½ to 2 pounds (0·67 to 0·9 kilograms) per week over the period of fastest growth. This is only a guide line and there is considerable individual variation but it makes the point that growth in puppies is quick and progressive. Any obvious check in growth rate should be a signal for close observation for any sign of departure from normal health. Sometimes the older puppy, say seven to nine months old may appear to be getting thin; this is often due to loss of the aptly named 'puppy fat' and the more rapid growth of skeleton. It can be deceptive but is often not a cause for concern.

CHANGES IN BEHAVIOUR

The growing puppy is very dependent until it is about five to six months of age and often appears to be very obedient at this stage. Gradual detachment and the development of a more independent 'teenage' behaviour pattern occurs when the puppy is approaching puberty (sexual maturity) which may be between six and ten months old. These changes in behaviour are perfectly normal. Displays of aggressiveness or bad temper are seldom related to ill-health and are usually a reflection of faulty training or a basically bad temperament, but irritability is occasionally shown by the puppy suffering from canine virus hepatitis (Rubarth's disease).

Changes in behaviour due to disease are more likely to be dullness, apathy, decrease in exercise tolerance, unwillingness to play and a desire to sleep for unusually long periods and if any of these signs develop and persist for more than a few hours you must seek veterinary advice.

LOSS OF APPETITE

Much the same remarks apply as for the young puppy but owners are sometimes worried that a pup which has hitherto enjoyed three or four meals a day is suddenly refusing one of them, usually the early morning or midday feed; this is no cause for concern but is merely an indication that the number of meals per day can be reduced. Failure to take several meals in succession or a persistent marked reduction in the amount taken, however, may well be a sign of illness and merits attention.

VOMITING

Dogs vomit very easily and the occasional vomit of bile (a yellowish, frothy fluid) often early in the morning, is not significant but repeated and/or severe vomiting is a signal that prompt veterinary attention must be sought because there are so many diseases of which vomiting is a feature and differential diagnosis may be exceedingly difficult. The cause may be extremely trivial, that the pup has eaten something which has irritated the stomach lining, or has over-eaten, or has had too rich a meal, but it may not be so simple. Once you realize that vomiting can be a feature of canine distemper, canine virus hepatitis, both types of leptospirosis, tonsillitis, and obstructive conditions of the alimentary tract at any level such as in the gullet (oesophagus), stomach, small intestine, or be a sign of some congenital anatomical abnormality, then the need for careful examination and diagnosis is obvious.

The veterinary surgeon will want to know a lot of things about this symptom, including how long it has been going on, frequency, whether its timing is related to a meal, if the appetite is good, what the material vomited is, for example, food (digested or not) or bile, if the pup retches before vomiting, and if the water intake is increased. If you have been observant enough to note these points it will be very helpful.

DIARRHOEA

The situation is similar to that with the young puppy except that in this age group nutritional causes, other than a sudden change of diet, are less likely to cause diarrhoea. Diarrhoea can be associated with viral and bacterial infection; of the former canine distemper is the most likely cause. Enteritis is not uncommon, sometimes accompanied by vomiting, and outbreaks often occur in a locality as a small epidemic.

You may occasionally see blood in the motion passed by a dog with diarrhoea, and while it is often not serious it is a sign that should not be ignored. If this symptom is repeated several times or in large amount, blood in the stool should be regarded seriously.

In addition to any drug treatment prescribed it is usual to recommend a controlled diet for several days. A commonly recommended regime is to withhold food for twenty-four hours, allowing frequent access to small quantities of water to which glucose has been added. Then a protein-free diet should be given for one to two days (that is, no meat, fish, cheese, and so on) for example, starchy foods such as rice pudding, arrowroot, cornflour, a little sweet biscuit or plain cake after which, assuming the diarrhoea has responded to treatment, a gradual return to normal over a further two or three days.

Diarrhoea in this age group can be caused by things other than infection, for example, eating substances which irritate but do not obstruct, such as chewing coal or coke or swallowing string or other textiles.

DISCHARGE FROM EYES AND/OR NOSE

As a rule a watery discharge from the nose is not significant, but if this becomes catarrhal or purulent (pus-like), then you must seek advice quickly because this may well be associated with an attack of canine distemper.

Discharge from the eyes may be due to local or general causes, that is, from the eye itself or its related tissues or as a sign of general (systemic) disease such as distemper. If there is an associated illness other symptoms will usually arise as well, such as cough, loss of appetite, and so on. Local causes are numerous and include the following:

conjunctivitis, inflammation of the mucous membrane lining the inside of the lids;

corneal ulcer, an ulceration of the surface of the eye;

inverted eyelids, (entropion) common in some breeds especially chow chows;

double row of eyelashes (distichiasis), which is also common in some breeds

such as poodles, and Pekingese;

abnormalities of the tear duct, common in poodles, especially white ones.

Once again, a single clinical sign can be associated with many different conditions, so again you need expert help.

COUGH

In the growing puppy coughing is most likely to be a sign of an infection such as canine distemper, 'kennel cough', or tonsillitis. Rarely, infestation with a minute worm which inhabits the lower end of the trachea (wind pipe) causes a persistent cough but this is one of the most unlikely causes. Dogs often end a coughing bout with apparent retching, and owners sometimes mistake coughing for vomiting.

The veterinary surgeon will want to know how frequent the coughing is, whether it occurs on change of temperature and atmosphere, whether it is loud or not and whether the dog seems to be trying to get rid of catarrh or phlegm.

Coughing may not always be serious but it should never be ignored because it is usually but one sign of some underlying condition which must be detected at an early stage if treatment is to be effective.

LOSS OF WEIGHT

With the exception of the apparent loss of weight when puppy fat is lost you should watch carefully if there is any change in body condition, and if it persists you should consult your veterinary surgeon. Some of the larger breeds, Alsatians in particular, may pass through a very lean period which may last until they are one-and-a-half to two years of age; if appetite is normal and there are no other abnormalities this often is just a question of late maturity. Veterinary surgeons are often consulted about such dogs and it is not unusual to find that they are very muscular but have little or no fatty tissue – nothing to worry about.

FRACTURES (broken bones)

There is nearly always some incident such as a fall, awkward jump, or a street accident prior to the onset of lameness, which is severe. Often the affected limb is carried, that is, it cannot bear weight at all or at best is only put very hesitantly to the ground. Surprisingly, after the first few minutes following the fracture, pain may not be very obvious, but a puppy that cannot bear weight on a limb thirty minutes to one hour after an accident should receive veterinary attention. This suggested time lag is to allow for a situation which can arise in the growing pup. The membrane covering bone, the periosteum, is very active in growing animals and has a large blood supply: if it is bruised, for example, following a knock, it is exceedingly painful and the pup refuses to use the limb but if there is no fracture the acute pain wears off quite quickly and a patient which initially showed many signs of having a broken leg may be quite sound within an hour.

Some fractures are fairly obvious and easy to diagnose, whereas others are very difficult and may require quite advanced X-ray techniques to detect them. Hence, veterinary advice is essential not only for accurate diagnosis but because treatment is clearly a matter for professional skill. The important rule is not to delay seeking advice in any case where lameness occurs suddenly, particularly if it is severe, and persists for more than one hour.

RICKETS

This is the rather general name which covers various abnormalities of growing bone. These bone dystrophies (faulty development) are seen most commonly between three and nine months of age but can also occur outside these limits. As a rule the pup shows signs of pain and lameness as well as a decreased willingness to exercise and play.

Sometimes the limb bones show enlargements at their extremities, especially near the carpus (wrist joint), but as such enlargements may be evidence of active growth, especially in large breeds of dog, as well as being a sign of rickets the problem once again requires expert help to resolve.

Should rickets be diagnosed it is almost certain that vitamin and mineral supplementation of the diet will be prescribed. Vitamin D is the most important factor concerned in bone growth but vitamins A and C can be involved as well. Mineral supplementation is usually given to supply extra calcium but the form in which it is given is also important. A word of warning – never give any additional vitamin source in addition to that prescribed; not only can excess of vitamins (particularly D) undo all the good that has been done but can actually cause abnormal bone growth as well! The balance of both vitamins and minerals is vital and should preferably be based on advice from your veterinary surgeon.

HIP DYSPLASIA

This is a congenital and hereditary condition of faulty development of the hip joints. It is very prevalent in some breeds, usually the larger ones, especially Alsatians, Labradors, and chows. It does not always cause lameness in growing pups but if it does it is likely to be present in severe degree. Signs to look for in pups of five months or older are difficulty in getting up from a lying position and a tendency for a rolling, swaying movement of the hindquarters especially on turning. Diagnosis can only be made by radiography.

The actual lesion in hip dysplasia is a badly formed socket of the cup-and-ball hip joint. The shallow socket results in a bad fit between it and the head of the femur and there is abnormal joint laxity which results in excessive movement. This in turn affects the moulding of the femoral head further affecting the socket, and so on. In addition, the joint reacts by producing new bone at certain edges. This is a form of osteo-arthritis, and in more severe cases can result in a quite young dog becoming crippled. Hip dysplasia exists in many degrees of severity, some so slight that there is virtually no effect on the dog throughout its life, others so severe that pain and lameness occur in young animals. Perhaps the worst are the medium degrees which cause no obvious lameness in earlier life but lead to osteo-arthritis in middle life or even sooner.

Unfortunately no treatment will rectify the faulty joint but there are surgical techniques (one very severe) which will alleviate pain in badly affected younger dogs but it must be clearly understood that these are palliative and not curative.

For these reasons owners want to know as soon as feasible if their dog is affected but diagnosis is far from easy in puppies except in the most severe cases. In fact, the official scheme for certification of freedom from hip dysplasia (run by the British Veterinary Association and Kennel Club jointly) is limited to dogs over one year old.

PATELLA LUXATION (dislocation of the knee-cap)

This is another abnormality which can be congenital and hereditary. It is commoner in small breeds such as toy poodles, Cavalier King Charles spaniels, Pomeranians, Yorkshire terriers, and so on. It is difficult to suggest the common signs of this condition but you may notice that the dog has a tendency to lift a hindleg and keep it flexed for a time before putting the limb to the ground again. In severe cases affecting both hindlegs there is obvious severe deformity of the limbs and a most abnormal gait, often likened to the hop of a frog or rabbit. In severe congenital cases considerable deformity of the limb bones can result with shortening of the patella ligaments. Not only does spontaneous cure not occur but the problem may worsen with age. This type of lameness usually requires specialized surgery which is undertaken with varying degrees of success.

SCRATCHING

The causes in this age group are very similar to those previously discussed. Most pups scratch occasionally particularly when changing coat, but frequent, severe scratching merits a trip to the veterinary surgeon unless some very obvious cause such as fleas or lice can be identified.

THE ADULT DOG

Many dogs, having been fully protected and boosted by vaccination against the infectious diseases in youth, will go through their adult years without ever needing veterinary attention. Much the same remarks apply as for the previous category but there are some additional warning signs which are more likely to be seen in grown dogs.

ABNORMAL THIRST

The water intake of normal dogs varies quite considerably, but generally dogs do not drink heavily. Pups up to four months old often do not drink water at all and thereafter the daily intake and timing of drinking is purely individual. It is important to note each individual dog's drinking habits and any prolonged change (other than one which can be attributed to obvious causes such as very hot weather) especially of an increased thirst should be watched and if this is associated with other signs you must seek advice at once. Even just an excessive thirst requires attention.

Polydipsia (excessive thirst) is a sign common to many diseases of dogs, some of them serious. For example, water intake is increased in kidney disease, diabetes, pyometra (a serious disease of the womb in bitches) and some forms of liver disease. In all of these diseases early diagnosis is essential so that you should never ignore this sign and you must obtain early veterinary advice. It may be very helpful to the veterinary surgeon to have a urine specimen for examination; try to obtain a sample of the first stream passed in the morning and put it into a very carefully washed container and take it to the surgery with the patient.

CHANGES IN URINATION PATTERN

Dogs urinate far more frequently than bitches because of their territory marking behaviour, but allowing for the difference between the sexes you should be able to observe any other changes. Increased frequency may be a sign of impending heat (season) in the bitch. If in either sex, however, there is increased frequency, apparent difficulty or excessive straining when passing urine, if it is passed only in small drops or the posture adopted is changed – this especially applies to males – or if blood is seen in the urine, there may be trouble in the bladder such as cystitis (inflammation of the bladder) or in the urethra (the passage between the bladder and the external orifice) and these require attention.

DISCHARGES

Any unusual discharge whether it be from eyes, nose, ears, anus, or the vagina of the bitch requires attention. In adult dogs there should not be any noticeable discharge from any of these parts except perhaps an occasional watery nasal discharge. The only other exception is a slight creamy discharge from a male dog's sheath, which is perfectly normal.

Other discharges, especially if catarrhal or purulent, should not be neglected. The possible underlying conditions are far too numerous to mention – it is enough to recognize that such discharge is abnormal and that advice must be sought. Don't try to guess at the cause.

Shaking and scratching of the ears,

To take the dog's temperature, firstly grasp the root of its tail to expose the anus; insert a lightly lubricated, stubby-ended thermometer from about 1 to 1½ inches (2·5 to 3·75 cm). Do not let go of the thermometer.

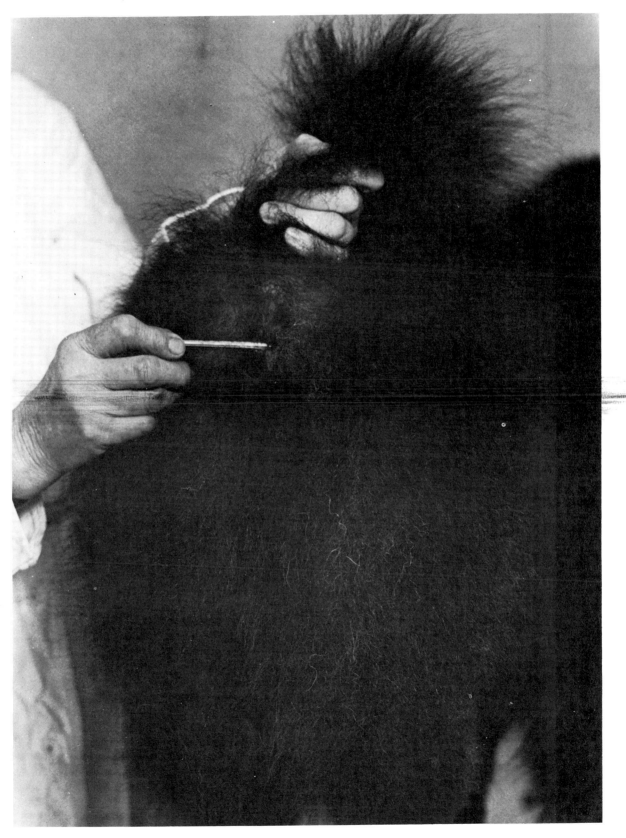

rubbing of the eyes or mouth usually indicate some form of irritation and if they persist this is not normal. There are many forms of external ear disease and the treatment will vary with the type present; attempts at home medication are seldom successful.

AGEING DOG

This is the age group where careful owner observation is so vital and it may be very difficult to distinguish between the normal limitations imposed by advancing years and evidence of ill health. Old dogs need more frequent, lighter, and more nutritious meals; they also need less exercise and this too should be little and often. On the other hand some of the diseases attributable to ageing can be treated if taken early and not allowed to proceed to an irreversible stage before advice is sought. Points particularly to watch for are changes in body weight, both decrease and a marked increase can be significant and should not be ignored. Once again an increased thirst for water is very important because so many of the geriatric conditions are characterized by this symptom. Loss of energy is another danger signal. It can be difficult to decide whether this is anything more than is to be expected in this age group but it must not be ignored.

While animals in the prime of life need not have regular health checks, occasional visits to the veterinary surgeon with the old dog as a precautionary measure are quite a good idea. Obviously this is something to be mutually agreed between owner and veterinarian but there are occasions when prevention is better than cure.

Coughing is another symptom which should not be dismissed too lightly in older dogs. It can be due to a variety of conditions but it is quite often a sign that wear and tear has caused a heart valve to become incompetent and if this is so treatment in the earlier stages can be most effective.

HOME NURSING

In these days of antibiotics and other 'wonder' drugs it is too often assumed that nursing is no longer important. This is quite untrue and it is a very lucky owner who does not have to nurse a dog back to health at some time during its life. If you are going to be away from the house all day, you should think very carefully before you buy a dog. Quite apart from administration of drugs a dog which is deeply attached to its owner will require frequent, reassuring attention to boost morale.

It can be a great help if owners learn to take their dog's temperature. This is done by inserting the thermometer into the animal's rectum; other methods, such as the skin under the foreleg, are quite unreliable. The stubby-ended thermometer is best for animal use and before insertion it should be lightly lubricated with petroleum jelly; whenever possible put the dog on the table with someone to pet it as a distraction. Grasp the root of the tail firmly and pull it gently upwards to reveal the anus; insert the thermometer, using some rotatory movement, for $1\frac{1}{2}$ inches (4 centimetres) into the rectum; hold it there for one minute, remove and wipe it clean with cotton wool; finally, read off the temperature. Do not let go of the thermometer because the dog will squeeze it out resulting in a broken thermometer. The average normal temperature for a dog is 101·5 °F (38·6 °C) but there can be variation. An excited or apprehensive dog can show a rise in temperature of 1·5 to 2 °F (0·6 to 0·8 °C) without any disease being present, and you should always take a dog's temperature when the animal is quiet after a rest, for example first thing in the morning. A bitch in whelp may, during the last three or four weeks of pregnancy, have a lower average temperature, 100 °F (38 °C), for example.

Home temperature taking can be a great help to the veterinary surgeon in monitoring the progress of a disease, and will be a guide if you are uncertain whether certain minor symptoms warrant professional help, – if the temperature is raised, they do.

It is too little appreciated how important it is to give prescribed drugs at regular, stated intervals. To be effective, a drug, whether given by mouth or injection, has to enter the body tissues and there reach and maintain what is called a *therapeutic level*. This concentration, especially in the blood, fluctuates in the interval between doses and it is important to keep up an effective, steady concentration. Two tablets at twelve-hour intervals will **not** be the equivalent of one tablet every six hours; more harm than good can be done by incorrect times and

When the dog requires medicine in tablet form, insert the thumb behind the large canine tooth (tusk) and press upwards on the roof of the dog's mouth. The dog will open its mouth so that the tablets can be dropped or pushed on to the back of the tongue.

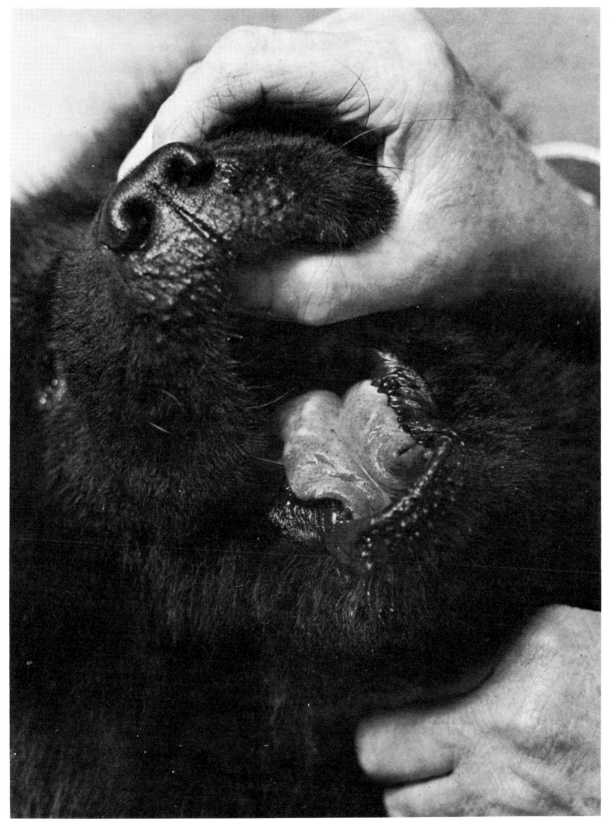

dosages. It is also important to give the complete prescribed course even if the symptoms have disappeared; it is quite usual to continue dosing for forty-eight hours after the animal appears normal. Veterinary surgeons usually dispense or prescribe the required number of doses to complete a course and this has been carefully calculated – it is not just a number thought up for fun!

Few owners these days will have the distress of nursing a distemper case because most dogs are vaccinated but if the new pet has been acquired from a home for stray dogs then it may well suffer an attack of distemper soon afterwards. Some distemper patients have a copious discharge from eyes and nose and this will require cleaning away very frequently.

It is often necessary to tempt a sick or convalescent dog's appetite, and little and often is the best way. Smell plays an important part in stimulating appetite so that foods offered should preferably have a fairly strong, attractive odour.

ADMINISTRATION OF TABLETS

Owners often think they can do it the easy way by concealing the tablet in a piece of meat or other food; sometimes this works but often it doesn't, especially if the patient has a poor appetite or is a fastidious feeder which will spit out the foreign substance. It is far better to give the tablet(s) and then you can be certain that it is done. Insert the thumb behind the large canine tooth (tusk) and press upwards on the hard palate; this will make the dog open its mouth and the tablet can then be dropped or pushed right over the back of the tongue; at once let the dog close its mouth and hold it closed until it swallows – if the dog doesn't swallow rubbing its nostrils or gently massaging the underside of the neck behind the jaw will often make it do so.

ADMINISTRATION OF LIQUIDS

These are often better given from a very small bottle than a spoon to save spillage. Pull out the hindmost corner of the dog's lips to form a pouch; gradually pour in the liquid, keeping the dog's nose tilted **slightly** upwards (not too far or it will start gagging)

so that the medicine trickles down into the throat behind the back teeth. Swallowing can be stimulated as before.

There are so many small things which go to making a sick dog more comfortable that it is impossible to list them all. It is, however, quite certain that even in this modern world nursing has an important part to play.

EMERGENCIES

Emergencies certainly do arise but the number of really urgent conditions with dogs is surprisingly small. No two people will agree completely on what constitutes a real emergency requiring veterinary attention as speedily as is feasible but the following list may help.

1 Accidents of all types; for example, road traffic accidents, falls, or severe damage in fights.

2 Severe haemorrhage (loss of blood) from any site, such as cut pads or leg, other wounds, blood in vomit or faeces (if not a single minor episode) or from the vagina or sheath. It is difficult to define severe haemorrhage because some people regard a drop or two as a disaster. A steady drip from a wound demands prompt attention.

3 Severe or repeated vomiting. This should not be allowed to continue for more than a few hours without attention; if the vomit contains much blood then even quicker help is needed. Dogs have a very sensitive centre in the brain which controls vomiting and they quickly acquire the 'habit' of vomiting even if the cause has gone, so that frequent vomiting may not be serious in itself, but may require some form of sedation to stop it.

4 Acute and severe diarrhoea. Seldom of desperate urgency but should not be allowed to continue for too long before getting help, especially if the motions contain blood. No more than twenty-four hours should elapse if the diarrhoea is really frequent.

5 Complications during whelping. The prudent owner will have warned the veterinary surgeon that their bitch is expected to whelp and give the dates. Most veterinary surgeons will give the owner some guidance as to when they should ask for help if things do not go normally. It is quite impossible to give brief guidelines on this topic.

6 Lactation tetany (milk fever). This is one of the few really urgent emergencies. It

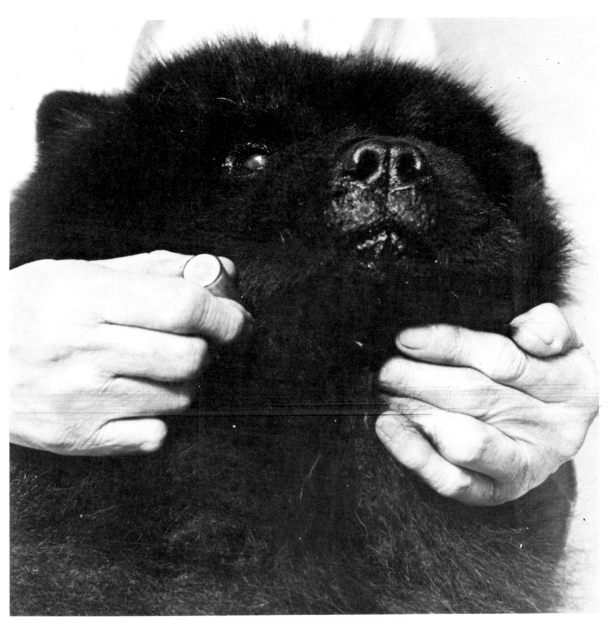

When the dog requires liquid medicine, make a pouch of the hindmost corner of its lips. Do not open the dog's mouth. A spoon or, as shown, a small bottle into which the dose has been measured, should be inserted into the pouch and the liquid allowed to trickle in.

arises in the bitch suckling a litter of puppies, usually between ten and twenty-one days old; it is due to withdrawal of calcium from body depots resulting in a sudden lowering of the concentration of calcium in the blood. Severe cases can be fatal in a few hours. The signs to look for are panting, trembling, and increasing weakness of the legs; the bitch loses all interest in the pups and may quickly become comatose. Treatment is completely effective but must not be delayed.

7 Recent ingestion (swallowing) of foreign bodies or poison. Occasionally, you may see a dog pick up and swallow something such as a small ball or stone, or eating poisoned vermin bait. In either case telephone the veterinary practice as soon as possible because it may be possible to recommend first aid measures over the telephone which could mitigate or avert trouble. Do **not** act without veterinary advice.

Owners, quite understandably often feel that immediate professional advice is vital in the case of fractures, fits, and heart attacks. Early attention is desirable, but it is not always quite so urgent as it seems. As previously mentioned, dogs with broken legs often do not suffer great pain unless

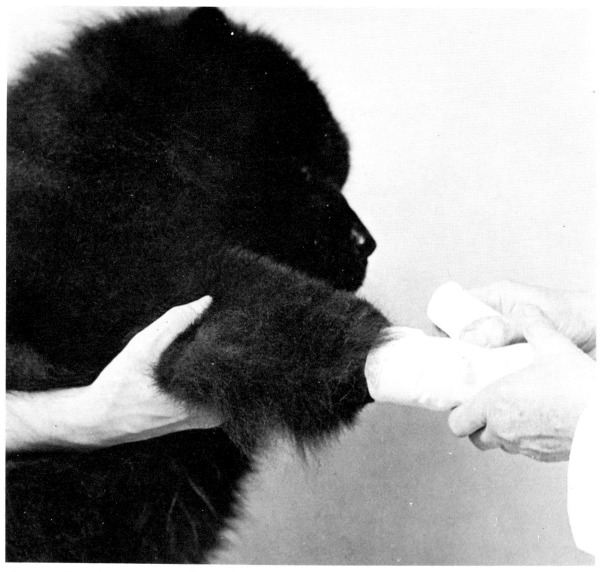

they are awkwardly moved and professional attention within a few hours may be quite adequate.

Fits and heart attacks are extremely alarming to the owner and often difficult to distinguish from one another. In the vast majority of instances the episode is of short duration, a matter of minutes, and is often over by the time veterinary help arrives. Curiously enough this may be an advantage because the most important thing is to decide the cause of the episode and this can only be done when the dog has apparently recovered.

A dog having a fit should not be restrained in any way. If possible remove furniture, and so on against which it could knock itself and darken the room; leave the patient strictly alone until it comes to the owner, obviously recognizing them and greeting them. The dog is not conscious during the convulsive stage, and there is no need to worry that it is suffering: it is far more distressing for the watching owner than the dog.

FIRST AID BY OWNERS

Unfortunately, the number of occasions on which first aid can effectively be given by owners is very limited but the following may be of some assistance.

1 Severe **haemorrhage** can arise from cut pads; it is fairly easily controlled in most

Above A pressure bandage is applied starting at the foot where it must be tightest. The dog's leg is held extended by a helper's hand behind the elbow.

Right In cases of severe haemorrhage from a cut below the carpus (wrist joint), tie a bandage as tightly as possible for no longer than twenty minutes. A *non-stretch* nylon stocking may be used instead.

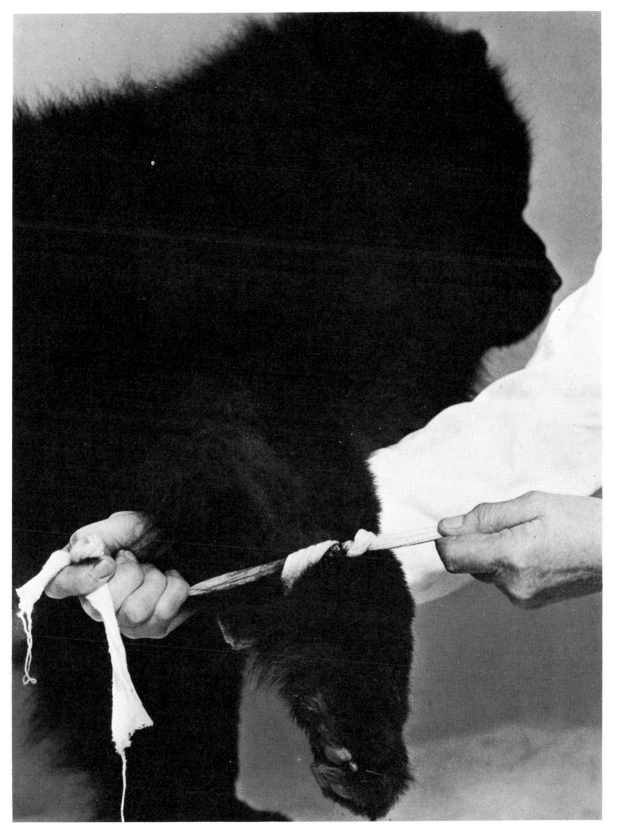

cases by applying a pressure bandage. This is a bandage applied to the foot, enclosing it and extending some 2 to 5 inches (5 to 12·5 centimetres) up the leg, put on in such a way that most tension is around the foot. This will usually be adequate until help can be obtained.

Perhaps the most serious place for a dog to sustain a cut is at the back of the pastern area of the forelimb, between the carpus (wrist) and foot; an artery can easily be severed in this area and pressure bandaging may not be enough – a stitch is often needed and this must be put in by a veterinary surgeon. If the bleeding is really copious it may be necessary to apply a tourniquet. A tourniquet applied to the leg above the cut is not always effective because the artery is now deeper in the tissues, and as a last resort it may be necessary to put one above the elbow but if this is done it must in no circumstances be left on longer than twenty minutes during which time advice and help must be obtained.

2 **Bee** and **wasp stings** are very common in the summer months and are seldom serious unless they occur in the back of the mouth and throat causing much swelling. Dogs should not be encouraged to snap at flies, wasps, and so on. You will not often know whether the sting is by a bee or wasp and it is simplest to use something which will be helpful in both cases, that is, bicarbonate of soda. This can be dissolved in water and used to bathe the affected area or can even be made into a paste and wiped on to areas such as the lips. The sting, if it is still in, should be removed.

3 **Scalds** are commoner than dry **burns**. Dogs are best kept out of kitchens when you are cooking and washing. If hot fluid does scald a dog it can be most deceptive because often there is apparently no damage and it is only some days later that the true condition shows itself. There is remarkably little that can be done as first aid but immediate dousing of the area with cold water will limit thermal (heat) damage to the tissues. Even if there is no obvious sign of skin damage, you should seek professional advice as soon as possible.

4 Certain breeds with shortish muzzles and restricted breathing passages are liable to **heat stroke** in hot weather under conditions of stress, such as at shows or, most commonly, shut in cars with inadequate ventilation. You must never shut a dog in your car in sunny weather. The temperature inside a car, even with some ventilation, rises alarmingly rapidly to very serious, even fatal, levels.

Dogs can sweat very little through the skin, so that they control their body temperature by heat loss through the tissues of the respiratory tract and mouth. If heat production exceeds the dog's ability to lose heat, heat stroke will result. The rectal temperature rises dramatically to anything between 107 and 110 °F (42 and 43·5 °C) and death or permanent brain damage can occur very quickly.

First aid is vital and comprises removal of the dog to a cool, shady, well-ventilated place and continuous dousing with cold water, either under a tap or from a hose. This treatment of the dog may need to be continued for one to two hours, until body temperature has returned to within normal limits.

5 **Asphyxia** can result from throat obstruction. Very occasionally a dog playing with a small ball will catch it and it will lodge in the back of the animal's throat. Asphyxia will quickly follow and there is as a rule no time to get veterinary help. Every attempt must be made to remove the ball which, because it is smooth, can be difficult. Holding the dog's head downwards or squeezing from outside the throat in an effort to dislodge it into the mouth may prove effective.

Even more rarely a dog swallows too large a piece of meat which may lodge similarly – the procedure is the same.

It is always unwise to try and grab a dangerous object with which a dog is playing because it may provoke the dog into an injudicious attempt to swallow it – a quiet approach is essential.

6 On rare occasions advice may be given to make a dog vomit after **swallowing a smooth foreign body**, for example, a ball or a stone, or some potentially poisonous tablets – such a step should *never* be taken without veterinary advice. The simplest way to make a dog vomit is to administer a small knob of ordinary washing soda, a piece varying from the size of a pea to a hazel nut according to the size of dog. Vomiting usually occurs within ten minutes and the offending substance may be returned.

Index

Numbers in bold type refer to illustrations

Murders,
and Mysteries

Crime flows through history like a muddied tide, flecked
red with the blood of murder. Murder is the most chilling,
the most fascinating of all crimes. Each killing leaves
traces: in forensic evidence, court reports, history and
folklore – and in more evasive, mysterious ways that seem
to speak to us from faded stains on ancient stones or
rusting fetters in long disused dungeons. Modern murders
may often seem casual and mindless, but history offers
many stories of mysteries, conspiracies and cold-blooded
killings, deeds so dark they stand out even against the
gloom of the grave and the shadow of the gallows.

Medieval Mayhem

Murder of the high by the mighty, assassination sanctioned by the lust for power, brutal bludgeonings in country lanes and town taverns; in the Middle Ages, murder was a sin most frequent. The punishment for murder, treason and a range of lesser crimes was death; for the traitor, death meant the protracted agonies of being 'hanged, drawn and quartered'. A populace inured to hard living and commonplace dying seldom wept to see wrongdoers chained, pilloried, flogged and hanged. For what was earthly suffering, compared to the torments of hell?

English historian Roger of Wendover gloated over the fate of Scottish patriot William Wallace, 'more raging in madness than Nero', who in 1305 was drawn through London 'at the tails of horses' to be hanged before 'his bowels [were] torn out and burned', his head cut off and his quarters carried north to be displayed as a warning to all 'rebels'. His was the ultimate penalty. Lesser punishments included the ducking stool (for nagging wives) and the pillory; offences for which a person might be locked in the pillory included selling stinking eels or underweight sacks of coal, gaming with loaded dice, forging a letter and picking pockets.

Strangers were regarded with suspicion, and generally barred from entering towns after dark, when at least 'two good men' stopped anyone wandering the streets with a weapon (unless he was a nobleman). Busy towns kept six watchmen on each gate. Travellers feared ambush by robbers, so much so that in 1285 King Edward I of England decreed that highways be kept clear of ditches and bushes for 200 feet (61 metres) either side, so that 'no man may lurk to do hurt'. A fleeing criminal was pursued with the 'hue and cry', everyone joining the manhunt.

The king's justice was dispensed by judges, sitting at 'assizes', a system of courts that survived into the 20th century. However, lawyers were held in low esteem; the 14th-century poet John Gower dismissing them as dogs scrabbling for 'the silver that is given them'.

ABOVE: Hugh le Despenser was executed at Bristol in 1326 for treason. His innards, having been 'drawn', are about to be burned. The Despensers, father and son of the same name, ran England during the last years of Edward II's reign (1307–27). Their greed outraged the barons, and Queen Isabella whose return in arms with her lover Roger Mortimer spelled their downfall. Gory execution followed.

ABOVE: The humiliation and discomfort of the pillory, in a French illustration of the 13th century.

PIEPOWDER COURTS

Held at fairs – 'piepowder' came from the French for 'dusty footed' – cases at these courts were judged by merchants. Not every miscreant was punished savagely. In 1291, at St Ives, 10-year-old John, 'son of Agnes of Lynn', escaped a whipping, or worse, for stealing a purse, and was told to go home and keep away from fairs.

TRIAL BY COMBAT
Divine judgement was sought in cases where there was a clash of evidence. Plaintiff and defendant fought, under fixed rules. If the accused won, he was innocent. If he lost, he was guilty — and if still alive, might be hanged.

ABOVE: *Nothing aroused medieval passions more violently than allegations of witchcraft and ritual murder. In 1144, a Norwich boy was allegedly murdered by Jews in a 'blood ritual', according to a local monk, Thomas of Monmouth. The Church made 12-year-old William of Norwich a saint, though his cult was later disavowed. This rood screen in St John's Church, Norwich, shows the saintly victim.*

ABOVE: *William Rufus, the second Norman King of England, was shot while hunting in the New Forest. Was it murder or accident? Chief suspect was Sir Walter Tirel (often spelled 'Tyrrel') who left the scene at the gallop, in guilty flight or to fetch help after loosing an arrow at a deer — and missing.*

3

The cathedral at Canterbury, England's cradle of Christianity, was stained by murder in 1170, and most shockingly by the slaughter of its own archbishop, Thomas Becket. Once the second most powerful person in the realm, Becket, a merchant's son, had fatally fallen out with his king, Henry II. It was not uncommon for kings to remove irritants and rivals – a nod in the right direction was usually enough, but for a high churchman to be so bloodily despatched was sensational. Becket had returned from exile to defend the Church against royal domination; outraged, Henry called him traitor and four 'enforcers' from the court in France hurried to England to exact vengeance.

Becket was hacked to death by these four knights and a subdeacon, his last moments gruesomely chronicled. The fifth sword blow 'horrible to say, scattered his brains and blood over the pavement', and while the body still lay on the cold stones, people soaked up the blood on rags or scooped it into flasks, so great was their desire for relics of the martyred churchman. Murder immortalized Becket; his shrine at Canterbury attracted pilgrims and wealth in equal measure until the Reformation of the 16th century, when his tomb was despoiled by Henry VIII's looters.

ABOVE: This stained-glass window in Canterbury Cathedral shows Becket with hand raised in blessing. The murdered archbishop was canonized in 1173.

RIGHT: Exeter Cathedral's superb collection of medieval sculpture includes this boss in the centre of the nave, which depicts Thomas Becket's murder. One of the Archbishop's knightly assailants was a Devon man.

Violent death removed kings, as well as king's enemies. The list of monarchs who were murdered (or probably murdered) includes England's Edward the Martyr (978), William Rufus (1100), Edward II (1327), Richard II (1399) and Henry VI (1471), and Scotland's James I (1437). Edward II met his end at Berkeley Castle, a fortress that held its own horrors; in its dungeon, guards threw rotting animal carcasses into a well-like hole, to 'scent the air'. To further amuse themselves, they would toss in a prisoner, to rot among the offal.

Plotting and blood letting reached a deadly crescendo during England's Wars of the Roses, in the 15th century. Power-broking nobles such as the 'Kingmaker' Earl of Warwick lent their support, and private armies, to whichever royal claimant promised most. After Warwick was killed in 1471, victory went to the Yorkists. Edward, Duke of York reigned as Edward IV until 1483, when his brother Richard of Gloucester moved into the seat of power. His accession was clouded by mystery, and almost certainly, a double murder.

LEFT: *Edward II alienated most of the English nobility and his wife Queen Isabella, who abandoned him for her lover Roger Mortimer. They are unlikely to have shed many tears at his death.*

BELOW: *This is the room in Berkeley Castle, Gloucestershire, where Edward II was held captive before his murder in 1327.*

ABOVE: *Berkeley Castle, the Gloucestershire fortress where Edward II died – his screams allegedly ringing through the castle corridors.*

Tower and Torment

Richard III (reigned 1483–85) was an enigmatic mixture of darkness and light. He eliminated opponents ruthlessly, and was almost certainly present or close by at the death of Henry VI in 1471. When he took the crown, Richard whisked his royal nephews, Edward V (never crowned) and brother Richard, into 'protection'. The Tower of London became their prison. Last glimpsed playing through barred windows in the summer of 1483, the boys were probably murdered in August. Their shades mingle with the ghosts of many confined or executed within London's grim royal prison.

ABOVE: *Edward V and his younger brother Richard were held in the Tower of London for several weeks during the summer of 1483, before (as most historians surmise) they were murdered, possibly smothered in their beds by assassins hired by Sir James Tyrrell.*

ABOVE: *Princess Elizabeth passed through the Watergate, now known as Traitors' Gate, on Palm Sunday 1554 – less than eight years after her mother Anne Boleyn had lost her head.*

From the Tower's walls Gruffydd, Prince of Wales plunged to his death in 1244 while attempting escape from his English captors. On Tower Hill, jeering peasants in revolt in 1381 beheaded the Archbishop of Canterbury and the Lord Chancellor. And in the Tower George, Duke of Clarence and brother of Richard III, was drowned 'in a butt of malmesie' in 1478.

The Tower was the final resting place for a motley company of princes, pretenders, religious dissidents, over-ambitious nobles, and a few innocents entrapped in plots not of their making. Conditions were not always grim; torture was used rarely and only on 'commoners'. Great men incarcerated there enjoyed small luxuries – in Sir Walter Raleigh's 12 years in the Tower he converted a hen house into a distillery, to pass the time when not writing. But in the end he, too, lost his head.

Many illustrious prisoners trooped into the Tower during the Tudor era. Both Sir Thomas More (in 1535) and Thomas Cromwell (1540) were executed there. So were Anne Boleyn (1536), Catherine Howard (1542) and the Seymours (Thomas in 1549, Edward in 1552). The axe ended the 'nine days' reign' of Lady Jane Grey, declared Queen of England in 1553 by her father-in-law, the Duke of Northumberland. When supporters of Mary I rose against usurpation, poor Jane begged to go home, but too late: she and her husband went to the block in February 1554. Mary's sister Elizabeth came close to losing her head, but the rebel Sir Thomas Wyatt swore before his execution that Princess Elizabeth 'never knew of the conspiracy'. After Elizabeth became queen, in 1558, her reign was regularly punctuated by plot and counter-plot, and she was constantly guarded against the assassin's knife, pistol or poison cup.

ABOVE: *The Duke of Clarence was 'privily drowned' in a cask of malmsey wine, in one of the more unusual courtly killings pervading British history.*

LEFT: *Lady Jane Grey's execution in 1554, as painted by Hippolyte Delaroche (1797–1856). The teenager so briefly 'Queen of England' whispered that she could not see to place her head on the block.*

Daggers for Crowns

Scotland's history is rich in royal murders. Robert the Bruce was certainly guilty of manslaughter, if not murder, in 1306, when he stabbed John Comyn in a church at Dumfries. In 1437 James I was murdered at Perth by one of his many noble foes, Sir Robert Graham, and his young son, now King James II, was present at the 'Black Dinner' in the Great Hall of Edinburgh Castle in November 1440, when Scotland's Chancellor, Sir William Crichton, lured into his grasp William, 6th Earl of Douglas and his brother David. Earl William was only 15, David 13, but Crichton feared a Douglas coup. When the meal was over, the head of a black bull was placed on the table: a signal for guards to seize the Douglases. A mock trial was staged before 10-year-old James, after which the two youths were beheaded in the castle yard. In 1452, James II committed his own murder, stabbing the 8th Earl of Douglas during a dinner at Stirling Castle.

ABOVE: *In this intensely dramatic painting by John Opie (1761–1807) the Scottish queen's secretary, Riccio, is beset by his murderers, while Mary struggles vainly to save him.*

ABOVE: *Royal murderer James II blasted the Douglas family by victory at Arkinholm in 1460, but was then blown up during the siege of Roxburgh Castle by one of his own cannons.*

Scottish monarchs seldom reigned without incident and it is no surprise that intrigue swirled around Mary Queen of Scots, daughter of King James V. When she returned to Scotland from France in 1561, she disliked the weather, the food, John Knox (who preached Protestantism at her interminably) and the Scots nobles, almost to a man coarse and cantankerous. Quick to resent an outsider, they particularly loathed Mary's Italian secretary David Riccio, whose music and wit brought a whiff of continental nostalgia to the queen. On Saturday 9 March 1566, Mary (six months pregnant with the future James VI) was relaxing over supper at Holyroodhouse with Riccio and her ladies, when in rushed her husband Lord Darnley and other noblemen. Riccio was stabbed, dragged into the next room and brutally done to death, with 56 wounds left in his body.

Darnley's charms were shallow, and Mary's new love, the Earl of Bothwell – so most people believed – planned his murder in 1567. The killing was unusual even for such violent times: not dagger or poison, but a blast of gunpowder that blew up the house where Darnley was sleeping at Kirk o' Field in Edinburgh. Darnley and his servant staggered from the ruins, and were strangled by persons unknown. Mary consoled herself by marrying Bothwell, but the path she had chosen led only to misery: miscarriage, abdication, incarceration, intrigue and execution.

ABOVE: Chief suspect for the Darnley murder was James Hepburn, Earl of Bothwell (c.1537–78), lover and 'abductor' of Darnley's wife, Mary Queen of Scots. This ambitious nobleman ended his days, mad, in a Danish prison cell.

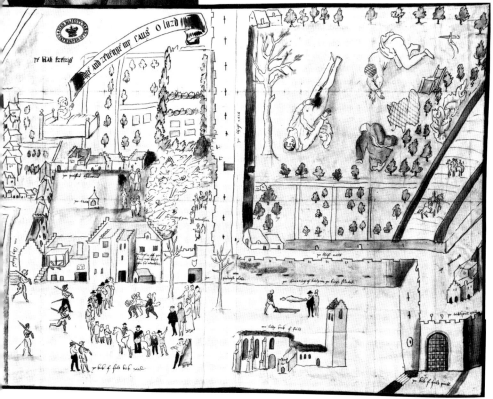

LEFT: A drawing from the time of the events at Kirk o' Field in 1567. Top left is the infant James VI; top right are the naked bodies of Darnley and his servant, with a chair, cloak and dagger beside them. The general view (left) shows the rubble after the explosion, and Darnley's body being carried away for burial.

Plots and Pretenders

Henry VII dealt briskly with two pretenders, Perkin Warbeck and Lambert Simnel. No wonder his son Henry VIII viewed the begetting of a legitimate heir as a matter of such urgency. Tudor monarchs' fears of treason at home and invasion from abroad were enhanced by Europe-wide violence between Catholics and Protestants. Elizabeth I, regarded in Catholic Europe as a legitimate target for assassination, lived in high security, guarded not only by her 'sea dog' sailors, but by a small army of secret agents, spies and informers.

Few assassins got close. In 1583 John Somerville, a 20-year-old Catholic gentleman 'affected with a frantic humour', made no secret of his plan to assassinate Elizabeth. He was arrested, and confessed, implicating his wife, his in-laws, and a Catholic priest who lived with them disguised as a gardener. Shortly before his hour of execution, Somerville was found strangled in his cell at Newgate, but his head was cut off anyway and, with his father-in-law's, set up above London Bridge. A similar fate befell Francis Throckmorton, another Catholic, who admitted under torture that he was in league with Spain to bring about an invasion of England, and was duly hanged at Tyburn in 1584.

Such precedents did not deter young Anthony Babington, devoted to Mary Queen of Scots since serving as her page. He belonged to a secret society aiding English Jesuits, such as Edmund Campion (executed in 1582). Charming but foolish, Babington agreed to head a conspiracy to make Mary queen in Elizabeth's place.

ABOVE: In his haste to kill Queen Elizabeth, would-be assassin John Somerville unwisely drew attention to himself but cheated the hangman by committing suicide.

This engraving by Cornelis Danckerts (c.1603–56) shows Anthony Babington and his fellow-conspirators, who hoped by killing Queen Elizabeth to restore Catholic rule in England.

THE PRICE OF TREASON

Traitors' deaths were prolonged and hideous: Anthony Babington watched one companion die before he too was hanged. He was still alive when taken down for the executioner to start work with a knife. Reports of his death agonies so moved Queen Elizabeth that she ordered the seven remaining conspirators hanged until dead, before the prescribed drawing and quartering.

Foolishly, he sent Mary details of the plan, and talked wildly at tavern suppers in London. Lord Walsingham's spies reported Babington's meetings and deciphered his secret letters. As the net closed, Babington fled to St John's Wood in disguise, cutting his hair short and staining his skin with walnut juice, but he was seized and, with six fellow-conspirators, went to the scaffold on 20 September 1586. The discovery of a letter from Mary to Babington, apparently approving his plan, sealed her fate. Within a year Elizabeth had signed her death warrant. The accession of James I in 1603 brought hope of less violent politics, but Catholic hopes of fairer treatment were swiftly dashed, and discontent planted the seeds of the most famous plot in British history, the attempt to blow up the Houses of Parliament in 1605. The public deaths of the gunpowder conspirators added another bloody chapter to the history of 'treason and plot'.

LEFT: *The execution of Guy Fawkes and other Gunpowder Plot conspirators in 1606. The prisoners were dragged behind horses to St Paul's churchyard. After his heart had been cut out, Sir Everard Digby is supposed to have gasped 'Thou liest' when the executioner held it aloft, declaring 'Here is the heart of a traitor'. Guy Fawkes died more quickly, his neck broken when he fell from the gallows ladder.*

Fire, Axe and Rope

ABOVE: *Burning destroyed the body: a fate thought most suitable for witches. Witch-burnings in Britain were rare, the last was in 1722 in Scotland. But in the reign of Mary I (1553–58), more than 250 people died in the fire for heresy. Women found guilty of treason, husband-murder, and counterfeiting died in the flames until burning was abolished in 1790.*

RIGHT: *The heads of executed traitors and conspirators were stuck on poles as a grim warning.*

Before the Norman Conquest of 1066, hanging was the usual form of execution in England. Beheading, ordered by William I for the execution of Earl Waltheof of Northumbria in 1076, became the convention thereafter for the nobility. Death was usually by the axe, though Anne Boleyn asked for a swordsman at her execution in 1536. Burning was a fate reserved for witches and those accused of religious 'crimes', such as heresy.

Hanging and burning were agonizing deaths. Decapitation could be near-instantaneous, though much depended on the skill of the 'headsman'. It took eleven chops to kill Margaret Pole, Countess of Salisbury, who at her execution in 1540 (aged 68) was chased around the scaffold by the inept axeman. A replica of the scaffold used at the execution of the Earl of Essex in 1601 can be seen in the Tower of London; on a low wooden platform, the condemned victim lay full length to place his or her head on the wooden block.

Hangings were popular; the diarist John Evelyn in 1664 wrote of 'seeing people flock in the City' to watch a London hanging, and paid a shilling 'to stand upon the wheel of a cart, in great pain, above an hour ...' while the condemned man eked out the time with 'long discourses and prayers' before being 'flung off the ladder in his cloak'. Remarkable mishaps included the story of Ann Greene, hanged for infanticide at Oxford in 1650, whose corpse 'came back to life' as a surgeon prepared to dissect it. In 1705, John Smith had been dangling from the gallows for 15 minutes when a reprieve came; it

SHORT DROP, LONG DROP

In a 'short drop' hanging, the victim was strangled, the convulsions adding to the spectacle. Hangman William Marwood tried the more humane 'long drop' in 1872, at Lincoln Prison. In his method, the prisoner fell between six and ten feet (two to three metres), so that the fall snapped the neck. The only man officially decapitated by the drop was Robert Goodale, hanged for murder at Norwich Castle in 1885. The hangman quit, blaming medical incompetence.

turned out to be a hoax, but 'Half-Hanged Smith' was duly pardoned. And in 1728 Margaret Dixon, after her hanging in Scotland, terrified onlookers by clambering from her coffin on the way to the cemetery.

Hangings remained public spectacles until 1868. Dickens wrote of his horror at the 'wickedness and levity' of the crowds: 28 spectators were crushed to death at a double hanging in 1807, and in 1865 an estimated 100,000 people watched Dr Edward Pritchard hanged in Glasgow. Hangman William Calcraft, who executed over 400 people between 1829 and 1874, carried out the last public hangings, at Maidstone in April 1868 of Frances Kidder (who drowned her stepdaughter) and at Newgate (May 1868) of the Irish Fenian Michael Barrett, who killed 12 people in an explosion at Clerkenwell Prison. The 20th century's busiest hangman, Albert Pierrepoint, succeeded his uncle Tom, who is said to have advised him: 'if you can't do it without whisky, don't do it at all'.

Albert Pierrepoint executed 433 men and women between 1932 and 1956, including the wartime traitors John Amery and William Joyce ('Lord Haw Haw'), and the Nazi war criminal Josef Kramer ('the beast of Belsen'). Among convicted murderers hanged by Pierrepoint were 'the acid bath murderer' John George Haigh in 1949, John Reginald Christie (of 10 Rillington Place) in 1953 and Ruth Ellis, the last woman to be hanged in Britain, in 1955.

Law and Disorder

An Italian visitor to England in the 15th century noted 'there is no country in the world where there are so many thieves and robbers'. Every day criminals were arrested, especially in London, 'yet for all this, they never cease to rob and murder in the streets'. Local constables were ill-equipped to fight serious crime while London's Bow Street Runners, ostensibly thief-chasers, were often suspected of operating on both sides of the law. After Sir Robert Peel set up the Metropolitan Police in 1829, similar forces were started nationwide. Plain-clothes officers made their appearance in the 1840s, and the Criminal Investigation Department (CID) in 1878. While crime detection was in its infancy, courts dispensed savage justice; flogging, hanging, penal servitude, hard labour and transportation to the colonies were meant to deter all but the most desperate criminals.

ABOVE RIGHT:
An imposing line of Victorian policemen, photographed around 1850.

RIGHT: Madeleine Smith, who may or may not have poisoned an obdurate lover. Speculation has continued ever since the jury in 1857 returned what is a uniquely Scottish verdict of 'not proven'.

The Victorians loved to read about murders. Poisoning was a 'classic' method and the trial of Madeleine Smith, in 1857, became celebrated. She was accused of murdering her fiancé Emile L'Angelier, and the verdict of 'not proven' left the case open to question. Madeleine was 22, and from a well-to-do Glasgow family; Emile, from Jersey, was a clerk; their relationship was clandestine and they became engaged in secret. After Madeleine's father introduced another suitor, businessman William Minnoch, the affair cooled; in January 1857, Madeleine accepted Minnoch's offer of marriage. She tried to break with Emile, but he refused and threatened to show her love letters to Mr Smith.

THE BODYSNATCHERS

In Edinburgh in the 1820s, William Burke and his partner, William Hare, made a lucrative living selling bodies to Dr Robert Knox and other anatomists. Burke got £7 10s 0d (£7.50) for his first corpse. The two then turned to murder, suffocating at least 16 victims and selling the resulting bodies. After their arrest, Hare gave evidence against Burke, who was hanged in 1829.

William Burke

William Hare

Madeleine carried on seeing Emile. After one meeting, he suffered severe stomach pains and sickness. On 23 March 1857, he was taken ill again and died in agony, apparently poisoned. The apothecary's poison book revealed that Madeleine had on at least three occasions purchased arsenic, saying she needed poison to kill rats. Her defence rested on the suggestion that Emile, the spurned lover, had killed himself, to shame or frame the woman who had rejected him. After the trial, Madeleine walked free, though not guilt-free, after a verdict of 'not proven'. She moved to London and eventually emigrated to America where she died in 1928.

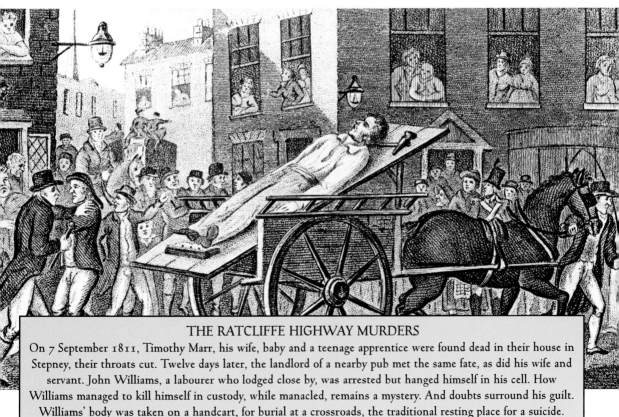

THE RATCLIFFE HIGHWAY MURDERS
On 7 September 1811, Timothy Marr, his wife, baby and a teenage apprentice were found dead in their house in Stepney, their throats cut. Twelve days later, the landlord of a nearby pub met the same fate, as did his wife and servant. John Williams, a labourer who lodged close by, was arrested but hanged himself in his cell. How Williams managed to kill himself in custody, while manacled, remains a mystery. And doubts surround his guilt. Williams' body was taken on a handcart, for burial at a crossroads, the traditional resting place for a suicide. A stake was driven through the heart. His skeleton was unearthed in 1886 by workmen excavating a gas main.

Assassins and Anarchists

From the mid 19th century, the British monarchy, and the Establishment in general, felt reasonably secure from the threat of assassination, after alarms in earlier decades. In 1812 the Prime Minister, Spencer Perceval, was murdered in the Palace of Westminster, and in 1820 the entire Cabinet escaped assassination by the Cato Street Conspirators, who hoped to start a radical revolution. After a 'mole' penetrated the conspiracy, the plotters were surprised in their hideout off the Edgware Road by Bow Street Runners on the evening of 23 February 1820. Five men, including the ringleader Arthur Thistlewood, were hanged; the rest were transported for life. Thistlewood announced from the scaffold, 'I shall soon know the last grand secret'; there were the usual cries of 'hats off!' from those at the back, eager for a better view.

Queen Victoria led a charmed life, surviving several attempts to shoot her by assailants usually described as deranged. But the violent anarchist and revolutionary politics of Europe impacted on Britain at the turn of the 19th century, *The Times* reporting that the East End of London harboured 'large numbers of very dangerous, very reckless and very noxious people', many of them exiles and revolutionaries on the run from the Tsarist police in Russia. In 1909, the 'Tottenham Outrage' hit the headlines when two 'foreign anarchists', known as Paul Hefeld and Jacob Lepidus, stole £80 in a wages snatch, and in a chase lasting over two hours fought a murderous gun battle with the police. The two commandeered a tram and a milk float, before shooting themselves.

ABOVE: *John Bellingham, a failed merchant, shoots prime minister Spencer Perceval in the lobby of the House of Commons. This print was published four days after the shooting on 11 May 1812.*

Two years later, another band of radicals tried to rob a jeweller's shop in Houndsditch by tunnelling from a nearby house, but aroused suspicion. When police came to investigate, three officers were shot and killed. The scene then switched to 100 Sidney Street, Stepney, reported to be the gang's lair. On 3 January 1911, the street was sealed off, and Home Secretary Winston Churchill arrived to supervise a siege by over 200 armed police and soldiers. Shots were fired, and the siege ended, after 10 hours, with the building on fire and at least two men dead inside. The mysterious anarchist 'Peter the Painter' (Peter Piatkow) may have been one of them, though other evidence suggests he escaped to America. Eight people were arrested, but only one found guilty, and her sentence was later quashed – Nina Vassileva lived in the East End of London until her death in 1963. By the 1960s, East End criminals tended to be less political, but even more violent – their models were the Kray twins and other gang leaders who ran 'organized crime'.

LEFT: *Roderick Maclean fires at Queen Victoria as she drives in a carriage through Windsor in 1882. Two Eton schoolboys drove back the 'lunatic' with their umbrellas. After this, the seventh attempt on Victoria's life, she commented, 'It is worth being shot at, to see how much one is loved.'*

MANHUNT 20TH-CENTURY STYLE
The new invention of wireless telegraphy helped trap murderer Dr Hawley Harvey Crippen in 1909. Having poisoned and cut up his wife, Crippen fled with his mistress Ethel le Neve (disguised as a boy) by steamer to Canada. The ship's captain became suspicious and alerted police by wireless; detectives crossed the Atlantic in a faster vessel, and arrested the pair at Montreal. Crippen was hanged.

ABOVE: *The Tottenham anarchist murderers make their getaway. This drawing was based on the account of tram conductor Charlie Wyatt, forced to drive with a gun at his head, as the other gunman swapped shots with pursuing police.*

BELOW: *Winston Churchill peers around a corner as armed police and soldiers stake out Sidney Street in London. Residents charged spectators 10 shillings (50p) a head to watch from rooftops and windows. Scenes of siege and stand-off were to become more familiar in cities during the 20th century.*

Scenes of Crime

Murder scenes range from the suburban to the desolate. In the 1960s the Moors murders, committed by Ian Brady and Myra Hindley, suffused Saddleworth Moor in Lancashire with a new and dreadful aura. Number 25 Cromwell Street in Gloucester is remembered for the sex crimes and murders committed there by Fred and Rose West in the 1970s and 1980s – though the house itself has been demolished. A nondescript doctor's surgery in Hyde, Cheshire, became notorious as the workplace of Britain's most prolific serial killer, Harold Shipman, convicted in 2000 of 15 murders, though responsible for many more deaths.

Murder leaves memories, even when a locality changes so much that few buildings or even street patterns remain. People still walk Whitechapel, lured by the horrific fascination of the Jack the Ripper murders in 1888, for no murder is so intriguing as the unsolved one. Fewer tourists strolling through London's Belgravia recall Richard John Bingham, 7th Earl of Lucan.

ABOVE: Lord Lucan: Eton, Coldstream Guards, father of three children, banker and gambler. Murderer? Or a victim of incredible coincidences?

Saddleworth Moor in Lancashire, indelibly associated with the sadistic crimes of Ian Brady and Myra Hindley.

'Lucky' Lucan, elegant gambler at John Aspinall's Clermont Club, was by 1973 down on his luck. His marriage was rocky, and he left his home and three children, complaining that his wife was insane. He had mounting money problems. In November 1974, Sandra Rivett, the Lucans' nanny, went downstairs to make tea. She was battered to death, and her body stuffed into a mailbag. When Lady Lucan came to investigate some 15 minutes later, she too was attacked, but (she told police) confronted her assailant – her husband, who admitted killing the nanny by mistake. The couple went upstairs, blood-spattered, before she slipped out to a nearby pub for help. The police found Sandra Rivett's body, a length of lead pipe, much blood, and upstairs two children asleep while an older child watched TV.

Lord Lucan vanished into the night. His car was found on 10 November, at Newhaven in Sussex; it contained incriminating forensic evidence, and more lead pipe. He was allegedly seen that night by a friend in nearby Uckfield, and phoned his mother. His version of events was that he had surprised an intruder, but feared his wife would accuse him. In letters Lucan said he planned to 'lie doggo for a while' after 'a traumatic night of unbelievable coincidences'.

ABOVE: *Murders by 'a Perfect Savage'. These words were spoken by the coroner at the inquest on Ripper victim Martha Tabram (killed 6 August 1888). The squalor of the murder scenes in London's slums, the sad lives of the victims (all prostitutes), and the sheer messiness of the killings cast a horrific shadow across the many and colourful theories about who the killer might have been.*

The coroner's inquest named Lord Lucan as the murderer of Sandra Rivett – the last time an English coroner named a murderer, as the law was changed shortly afterwards. But Lucan had become the most famous disappearing man of modern times. Lucan lookalikes were reported from around the world but in 1999 he was declared dead by the High Court. Had he drowned, or fled abroad? Did he plan to kill his wife and did the plan go terribly wrong? Was there a mysterious 'intruder'? The jury is still out …

ABOVE: *Dr Harold Shipman, Britain's most prolific killer? His victims certainly numbered over 200, most of them elderly patients.*

LAST TO BE HANGED
The death penalty for murder was abolished in Britain in 1965. The last hangings were on 13 August 1964, when Gwynne Owen Evans was hanged at Strangeways Prison (Manchester), and Peter Anthony Allen at Walton Jail (Liverpool); both had been found guilty of murder in the course of robbery.

Secret Wars

Crime today may be subtle and hidden, as in computer fraud. But it can also be stunningly public, in both action and consequences. The assassination of an Austrian archduke in 1914 kick-started the world to war, while the 9/11 suicide attacks in the United States in 2001 polarized opinion as few other events in modern times.

In the 21st century, the battle against crime and terrorism is international, a war fought not just with guns, but through informers, electronic bugs and high-tech surveillance via mobile phones, TV and the internet. As intelligence-gathering becomes ever more complex, our freedom and privacy is arguably eroded by intrusive state power, media manipulation and electronic snooping. Crimes of passion or murder for money are no longer so shocking, society's fiercest condemnation being reserved for the child murderer. Gangland killings still stain the streets, but the news is more often dominated by political assassination, 'ethnic cleansing' and mass terror on a scale unimaginable to earlier generations. The attack at Omagh in 1998 and the London bombings of 2005 killed innocent people going about their everyday lives. Such crimes make life seem less secure and so even more precious.

In a dangerous world, the appeal of 'old-fashioned' mystery and murder stories is understandable. No wonder crime fiction has continued to sell so well, ever since the first fictional detectives stalked the bookshops in the 19th century. History, like fiction, is enlivened and enriched by tales of intrigue, conspiracy and the battle between good and evil – a struggle as central to human life now as it was when history was first written, and murder first planned.

RIGHT: Austria's Archduke Franz Ferdinand and his wife are shot by Serbian nationalist Gavrilo Princip; Sarajevo, 28 June 1914. Political murder never had more costly consequences. The First World War had begun by 4 August.